DARLENE S. WATSON

A STORY OF HATE, LOVE AND FAITH

A STORY OF HATE, LOVE, AND FAITH

Pearly Gates
Publishing LLC

"Inspiring Christian Authors to BE Authors"

Pearly Gates Publishing LLC, Houston, Texas

A Story of Hate, Love, and Faith

ISBN 10: 1945117435
ISBN 13: 9781945117435
Library of Congress Control Number: 2016954058

For information and bulk ordering, contact:
Pearly Gates Publishing LLC
Angela R. Edwards, CEO
P.O. Box 62287
Houston, TX 77205
BestSeller@PearlyGatesPublishing.com

DEDICATION

This book is dedicated to my very best friend, Ann Tate, who was with me when I first fell apart from all of these memories. She has come to my rescue time and time again - many times, praying for hours and staying with me until it was over. She saw firsthand how bad it was, yet she never left me. Ann has gone through thick and thin with me for 40 years of my life. There aren't enough words to express what that meant to me. Thank you, Ann. I love you!

ACKNOWLEDGEMENTS

I want to first give all the glory to my Savior, Jesus Christ. Without Him, this book wouldn't have come about. It is really His story - not mine.

To my Son, John Fonseca: You went through a lot of pain because of what happened to me. I was crippled with fear most of my life, which stopped me from doing a lot with you. I know you missed out on a lot. Through it all, you still had my love. I pray you knew that beyond a shadow of a doubt. Thank you, John. Mom loves you!

To my Friend, Ann Tate, and her Goddaughter, Nikki Cheree: Thank you for holding to your word to help me. You connected me to a wonderful person, Angela Edwards, CEO of Pearly Gates Publishing. You are ALL making my dream come true! Thank you ALL!

To my Dear Mom, Audrey J. Conti, who I believe went through what I did, but much more severe: I love her dearly and I do understand why she was so sick all of her life. Because of her, all of her children and grandchildren have character today.

INTRODUCTION

My mission for this book is this:

For all those people who aren't free, I desire to help them turn to God. Know that He has a purpose for their lives. Through my story, I want to give them hope. If God can do this for me, He can do it for them.

~ Darlene S. Watson, Author ~

TABLE OF CONTENTS

Darlene S. Watson

A Cure for Shame

JeSUS

SECRETS MAKE US SICK LOVE HEALS

Darlene S. Watson

Joy of the Journey

I want to say: What a journey with the Lord this has been! It hasn't always been easy following the Lord, but it has been worth it. Each step of the way, He has revealed His character to me little by little. I've come to know Him more and more, and the more I know Him, I trust Him to take care of me. He helps me figure out what I'm about. It's not easy to face myself; in fact, it's very painful. We try to run and hide from ourselves...only to fall flat on our faces.

God is there to pick us up so we can know that without God, there's nowhere to go. We think so bad of ourselves that we don't give God a chance. God wants to show us what went wrong, then He helps to make us strong. We're so afraid of what we'll see, we don't take the time to be set free. When we focus on what God can do, He makes us brand new.

You have to be willing to come to the end of yourself to know yourself - like God knows you. He, after all, created us and knows what's hidden in the dark. We're not all made the same. He's put in each of us our own unique selves. We so often compete and compare ourselves to others, we're not aware of who we really are. I want to know my purpose. I want to find out what makes me tick. It is a path of discovery, and we can't do it without God. He knows me better than I do! There are things in me I didn't know and He tells me things that make me grow. I'm finding out that you can't control another: You can only control yourself.

A Story of Hate, Love, and Faith

When you are at peace with God and yourself, then you can be at peace with others. When you know that God has a plan just for you, you will want that to come true. People are always telling us what they think we should do and to always follow the crowd. How can people tell you what to do when they don't even know what's right for them? We're in life's school to be our very best and to learn lessons every day. A lot of things we think about ourselves can hinder us along the way. We are all in a race 'til God calls us home. Run your race the best you can. I want to end my life better than I started. The joy of the journey takes time!

Darlene S. Watson

Inside Out

I was looking in the mirror and didn't see me, but a little girl of two or three.

I shook my head to shake the delusion and when I looked again, I saw my confusion.

I didn't know who was taking control; me or the little one who was my soul?

I ignored a lot of her pain because when she was out, I thought I was insane.

She's out now for me to see. I can no longer ignore the child in me.

She was telling me how much she hurt - and when she could, clue words she's blurt.

Too many memories I wanted to hide. All it did was fester inside.

I don't want to silence her anymore; after all, she is my core!

I know now she's a part of me. I've got to help us to be free!

She knows me all too well because she is the reason I'm in a shell.

She's the one who fell apart when all the people broke her heart.

Now I see her in a new light. I know in time, we'll set things right.

She's still scared and living in the past. I reassure her, "It won't last."

More and more, her trust I gain. Little by little, it eases her pain.

Her terrors and fears are not as much. What settles her down is a loving touch.

It's still not easy to talk about, but when I do, she's glad it's out.

No more secrets we have to hide. It feels good to be happy inside.

And when there are days and my mind is reeling, she lets me know it's her I'm feeling.

I listen to her now because she's my guide. No longer will I keep her hidden inside.

Until we can mend what they did to our soul, she knows and I know we will never be whole.

Darlene S. Watson

All Shook Up

Grownups shouldn't do bad things to kids because sometimes in their lives, they pop their lids.

I had flashbacks that boggled my mind. Thank God for my friend who was so kind.

I didn't know I was out of whack. I tried and tried to bring myself back.

When my friend saw my face full of fright, she knew then something wasn't right.

I was reliving a scene I knew nothing about. I guess you'd say it was time to come out.

I was going down when my friend grabbed my head; not calling for calling, but praying instead.

After that, I came out of it…not talking a lot, just a little bit.

I try to be calm through all of this mess, but that's hard to do when I regress.

I had flashbacks that hit me all in one day. My scared friend didn't know what to say.

She learned a lot by watching me, that there really was a child that she did see.

She told me later everything I did; not as an adult, but as a kid.

I was acting out what my mind suppressed, and without warning, I regressed.

It's still hard for me to comprehend. I'm just glad God was with me…and my friend.

A Story of Hate, Love, and Faith

Nosy Me

I was always around to hear the scoop. That's why I called myself "Whoop the Snoop".

I would listen to them an awful lot and wouldn't give in, but because they were so big, they knew they would win.

They made threats not to tell, and if I did, I'd burn in Hell.

I would get worked up with so much fear, that half the time I couldn't hear.

They'd laugh at me when I'd scream the most, then they would gather around and make a toast.

"Little girl, little girl, don't make a sound. Don't forget: We're always around."

I tried my hardest to be tough, but they were strong and real rough.

I couldn't stand all of their touches, but I couldn't escape from their clutches.

I was out one night being a sneak; all I wanted was to take a peek.

What I saw made me sick! I took off really quick.

My heart was pounding and I couldn't think. All I could do was blink and blink.

Whoopy Snoopy got us into this mess - sneaking around - that's why they were trying to break me down.

After they were done, I forgot what I saw. All I could do was bawl and bawl.

I made a promise (when I stopped crying) that I would stop my night spying.

Even though I stayed out of their way, they did things to me anyway.

I loved to bust them when they were wrong - and when I did, I felt strong…

Darlene S. Watson

The Stalker

Fear is my stalker day and night. I wish I knew how to get rid of this fright.

He thinks he's smart - scaring me like this. Peace of mind I sure do miss.

I noticed a lot when he's around. It's hard for me to get my ground.

He makes me think there's no hope, and gets a thrill when I can't cope.

I wish I knew how to get rid of him. I'm sick and tired of seeing things grim.

Because of him, I'm scared to death…always thinking I'm taking my last breath.

I can't even drive without him there; it's no fun…just one big scare!

He makes it so I don't get rest. He knows then he's done his best.

He's everywhere I look when things are bad. When I can't shake him loose, I get mad.

I wish I knew what he's about so I can work on getting him out.

Gloom and doom is all he knows; scary things he loves to show.

I try to fight him, but he's too strong. I'm just too weak when things go wrong.

He's on his guard, ready to strike; happy thoughts he doesn't like.

I pretend he's not with me so he'll go away. When that doesn't work, I start to pray.

For a while, he leaves me alone; then he's back blowing his horn.

He's always been with me for as long as I can remember. I just wish he'd give up and surrender…

A Story of Hate, Love, and Faith

My God

On my hill, it was just me. I was alone - and so was He.

I felt so good when He was around, even though He didn't touch ground.

When He was with me, I had no doubts because He would tell me what He was about.

I was trying to understand what He was telling me; all I remember is, "Think of Me".

He was telling me He was always near; my cry for help He'd always hear.

Even though He was out of sight, He's the One who helped me fight.

He kept a lot I couldn't bear, and these were things He didn't share.

When I was in pain that was too much, He'd be there with His loving touch.

The pain wasn't so bad when He was there. He gave me strength so I could bear.

I always told Him everything; a load off my shoulders it would bring.

I knew where He lived because He took me there when the pain was too much to bear.

I wanted to stay with Him, but He explained it wasn't my time; He told me that with Him, I'd be fine.

I didn't want to go back to all of that pain, then He told me He'd see me again.

He told me, "It is a test of all time. If you believe in me, you'll be mine."

God was His name. He told me, "You'll know me - if you believe".

He talks to me when I am down, letting me know He's around.

I felt unclean when they took me at will. After that, I stopped going to my hill.

I didn't want God to know what they did to me and why I felt unworthy of Thee.

He was always there through thick and thin. That's because I always believed in Him...

A Story of Hate, Love, and Faith

Alone

I feel she doesn't care when she denies their part. She holds me back from making a clean start.

There's only so much I'll let her know, only because I love her so.

Our relationship is different with each other; what stands in the way is her brother.

I can't really talk about all of this; someone else is the one, she insists.

I go along and let it be, knowing then: She doesn't believe me!

It hurts me so bad that she takes their side, and all of this she wants to hide.

I'm her child and they, her family. She takes their side over me.

They deserve to be exposed for what they did. They're the reason I flipped my lid!

I wouldn't protect them - no siree. I'd tell in a minute if it were me.

I believe the truth will set you free; if this keeps up, she'll hear from me.

When it comes out about my past, every one of them I will blast.

I feel like I don't exist, only because I'm alone in this.

I need someone who can relate; my true feelings I want to state.

I protect my mom the best I can. I don't know how much more I can stand.

Nothing's right nor the same; they're the ones I still blame.

Mom doesn't mean to do this to me; she just can't accept it was her family…

Darlene S. Watson

Ouch

There are days I can't get out of bed. Too much pain is in my head.

They scraped me good and hurt my guts; boy, oh boy - were they all nuts?

They tied me up by my wrists; I still get a little twitch.

It's hard for me to go number two. That's the place they invaded, too.

They tortured me in all places. They were smart to leave no traces.

My arms hurt in different spots. That's from being hung up a lot.

My hands go numb from the rope they tied. I couldn't run - even if I tried.

The pain in the back of my head won't go. That came from a heavy blow.

When they shut the lid, pain in my neck I couldn't rid.

My back has spasms in the night. That was from all my fright.

I always feel I am hunched; in a small space I was crunched.

On my leg, I feel a welt. That was from a heavy belt.

My arms go limp when I lift them high. That came from being in the sky.

Cramps in my back from hanging on; I didn't want to hit the ground.

The jack in the box hurt my bones; I was in there all alone.

My body is feeling the pain I felt then. I just want it all to end…

A Story of Hate, Love, and Faith

Rattle On

Always drunk, grabbing at me. Creepy crawlers are what they'd
be.

Party-hearty, they did well; seeing the mess, you could tell.

They drank morning, noon, and night. They sure were a dreadful
sight.

They fought with each other; it didn't matter if they were sister
and brother.

Too much to drink made them mumble and sometimes, they
would even stumble.

They made fools of themselves time and again. Early in the
morning they'd begin.

Drunks were saying sick things to me. I couldn't stand it when
they wouldn't let me be.

They told us kids to go and play. They just wanted us out of the
way.

Camp is where this all took place; they had beer by the case.

I couldn't get too much sleep because always around was a
creep.

I liked it when they were out of it; a lot of information I would
get.

I'd keep it stored in my head and sort it out in my bed.

They'd say things that didn't make sense; when I was around, I
was always tense.

I'd play dumb to fake them out so I could hear what they were
talking about.

We always ate peanut butter and jelly. That wasn't enough for
my little belly.

When they cooked, it was always late. I ate everything on my
plate.

They'd laugh and snicker from all that liquor.

I didn't like the creeps around, but every weekend they would
come down.

Darlene S. Watson

Lost and Found

I'm scared out of my mind 'cause my mom, I can't find.

Crazy people all around. I don't like the scary sound.

Pat and me were given away; this is where we had to stay.

I was holding onto the gate trying to be calm. All I wanted was my mom.

Pat was real scared; he held on to his little bear. Please, please come for us; mom's the one we both trust.

They pressured grandma into doing this. Leave her alone, I would wish.

My uncle was behind all this; he's one person I wouldn't miss.

I was told my mom wanted this. She couldn't handle all of us kids.

When we were allowed out to play, at the gate I would stay.

On the pillow where I slept is where all my tears were kept.

Pat didn't think much of it; he just thought we were there to visit.

People would come up and scream in my face. I wanted out of this crazy place!

I would be strong for Pat's sake. Funny faces I would make.

I would sing lullabies and wipe the tears from his eyes.

I cried and cried when I was alone; all I wanted was to go home.

I was so sick, I couldn't eat. Half the time, I wouldn't speak.

I was Pat's mom while we were there. I told him often how much I care.

In my sleep, I would dream. I'd wake up from my scream.

I walked around like a zombie; all I wanted was my mommy.

A Story of Hate, Love, and Faith

Mad as Hell

So I wouldn't tell what you wanted to hide, you tried to get on my good side.

I didn't like it when you fooled my mom and acted so fake when she wasn't around.

I always tried to be alert because I knew how you could hurt.

I was on the stairs ready to jump; when you wouldn't catch me, I fell in a hump.

When I got up, you were laughing at me. That made me mad because you were picking on me.

I was tied to a table begging for my life; the woman who scraped me was your wife.

You weren't alone when you ripped me apart; there was four of you from the start.

"The devil's child", you kept telling me - because that's what you wanted me to be.

When I'd break my trance that I was under, your voice would boom and sound like thunder.

You were always around because you lived there; I never liked your mean stare.

The cellar was where you locked me in. That's when my fear was sinking in.

You put me in a box made of steel and shut the lid so I wouldn't squeal.

I was shaking so bad; I couldn't calm down. All I thought was, "I hope I'm found!"

You tied me up like a pig, close to the fire that was lit.

You tortured me in your day, but I'm the one who has the last say.

I'm not little anymore. You could say I'm settling the score…

Darlene S. Watson

Secrets

Power from the devil is what you seek. Cruel words and lies you all speak!

They were my uncle and my aunt; "Devil's child!" they would chant.

They had to sides no one seen. One was the leader, and one was the queen.

They're not human to do all that. They're the devil - that's a fact!

They took a child that was so bright and filled her up with terror and fright.

They'd laugh at her when she was in pain, really trying to drive her insane.

They brainwashed me not to tell. That's how they had me under their spell.

When grandma was sleeping and out of sight, they would worship the devil late at night.

They would sacrifice animals with a full moon; it had to be then and not too soon.

They had a church that wasn't grandma's teaching. All you could hear was the devil preaching.

When they were dressed in different disguises, they would have all kinds of surprises.

"God" was one he likes to play; he's the one that zapped me away.

He would always mix bad and good; I'd tune him out whenever I could.

"God" was always around to pounce on me because I'd tell grandma the things I'd see.

She would read the Bible every day, just to keep the devil away.

Their masks were ugly and scary, too - but I still know all of you...

See Me

Can't anyone see what's wrong with me? After what they did to me?

There were days I'd stare in space; all the time, my heart would race.

I'd walk around in a daze and see everything in a haze.

I'd throw up and couldn't eat. Couldn't anyone see me?

I couldn't get out of bed half the time. Can't they see I'm not fine?

I was jumpy when they were around. I wouldn't dare make a sound.

I moped around so they would see; all they did was pass by me.

I shook a lot out of fright. No one asked, "Are you alright?"

I would double over in severe pain. My bad nerves were the blame.

You know better than to make up things. That's what telling on them would bring.

When I was scared, grandma's hands I'd clutch; but she was too old and couldn't do much.

With the pills they made me take, laughing sounds I would make.

I'd be so high, I couldn't talk. It was hard to even walk.

Even though it was my grandma's house, my aunt and uncle took charge of us.

They were mean to my grandma as well. She was also scared to tell.

Nobody cared what I was going through.

Don't tell me no one knew!!!

Darlene S. Watson

Satan

Satan was a powerful man - someone who I really couldn't stand. He had eyes that glowed in the dark; he got pleasure, ripping dogs apart.

He had followers who were just like him. I used my mind not to let them in.

He mixed good and bad. When he talked about God, I got mad.

"We'll pretend we believe in God so nobody will know, but don't tell them we told you so."

He'd come get me late at night. I was too sleepy to put up a fight.

He had sis help him a lot; what I didn't want to see, I'd block.

We worshipped Satan (as you can see); now all three repeat after me.

They were spooky…all dressed in black. Why, oh why, do they believe in that?

"He's our power. Believe in him. It's not new; it's always been."

As God, He did bad things, too; I didn't know who was who!

They wore masks to hide their faces. They did scary things at different places.

We couldn't run because of him. Our chance to escape was real slim.

He was such an evil man; when sis untied me, we both ran and ran.

When I got a chance, Satan I would bust. He wasn't someone you could trust.

A Story of Hate, Love, and Faith

Gone Mad

It's a black hole...I can't get out. Is anyone there to hear me shout?

It was dark and dirty, too; how to get out? I haven't a clue.

They buried me alive in a sack, so I couldn't find my way back.

He scared me to death and buried me alive. He didn't want me to survive!

I bawled and bawled while I was down there. It was too much for my mind to bear.

He scared me to death so it would sink in - how much he hated me...and I, him.

"The death of you yet!" he would say. "I'll make it so you won't see day."

I couldn't stand to see his face. I would look through him into space.

I was so petrified; I couldn't stop crying. All I could think about was dying.

He left me there for me to rot. All I thought about was death - a lot.

He scared me out of my mind; peace on Earth I wanted to find.

When he was around, he was always after me.

Now he's gone, and we can be free...

Darlene S. Watson

Don't Make Sense

I didn't want to be alone. I was scared right to the bone.

There wasn't anyone I knew there. All I saw was their blank stare.

My mom was in there with the rest. I was scared, but did my best.

I knew this lady all in grey. It was such a sad, sad day.

She was someone I knew once. I sure loved her a whole big bunch!

I didn't want to leave her there; her painful look I couldn't bear.

Actions speak louder than words to me. After all, I was only three!

I couldn't stay with her that night, even though I was full of fright.

We came to have lunch with her; loneliness inside she would stir.

It was such a bright, sunny day. I think it was the month of May.

She felt so good; I could burst! Seeing her in there was the worst.

When she wasn't with us, we felt alone. Can't you come with us so we can go home?

Grandma took our mom's place when mom left without a trace.

They told us that she didn't love us anymore, so don't stand there crying at the door.

Grandma washed our faces after that, then went to the chair where she always sat.

We sat down by grandma's feet; she was talking so soft and sweet.

"Your mom loves you very much", then she'd pat us with her touch.

Grandma was always there for us. She was the only one we could trust...

Clouds

When I needed peace, I'd look for them. Pretty pictures they would send.

We would gather on the hill. The day was bright; the sky was still.

They were white and fluffy, too. They look pretty against the blue.

My friends came out when days were bright; seeing them there, my mood was light.

All shapes and sizes my friends were. The best of friends - that's for sure!

They would listen to me day after day. I sure had a lot to say!

I felt better talking out loud. I'd look up to see my cloud.

My friends lift me up so I won't brood. They change their form to fit my mood.

They would float in the sky keeping me busy so I wouldn't cry.

They'd make faces to ease my pain. A peaceful feeling, I would gain.

One by one, together they'd form - just in time for a storm.

My friends got me through a lot of pain, and cried for me when it would rain.

Their shapes and sizes were so neat. With their help, loneliness I could beat.

They were friends close to me, they didn't have to say a thing.

I spent a lot of time visiting them…silent messages they would send.

They made me smile and laugh a lot, too. They were so soothing, you'd like 'em, too!

Grandma

Grandma had long, grey hair. It would fall past her chair.
We loved the fat on her arms and would play with them without harm.
We rubbed her legs so she could rest. We tried real hard to do our best.
She rubbed our backs and combed our hair. That was her way of showing she cares.
"Hark, hark!" she would say. "Now, you kids go out and play."
There really wasn't much to do, so we took naps with grandma, too.
We were so funny for grandma's sake; funny faces we would make.
She taught us about God every chance she could. "Always remember Him being good." We shook our heads yes and said we always would.
We would tell grandma a lot of funny things; a smile on her face we would bring.
Grandma would have us sing songs with her; happy thoughts they would stir.
Grandma would give us oatmeal and toast. She is the one we loved the most.
Then we moved away from her…the memory of that is still a blur.
We would visit her every year; it wasn't the same 'cause she wasn't near.

A Story of Hate, Love, and Faith

Love

God is with us even when things go wrong. Believe it or not, He makes us strong.

With His grace from above, He helps us through with His love.

And even though He's not in sight, He still tries to make things right.

When you're down and there's no hope, pray to Him to help you cope.

Just because He doesn't appear doesn't mean He doesn't hear.

A lot of people think because we don't see His face, that He left us without a trace.

That's why people don't look to Him when their lives are sad and grim.

Faith and trust we put in Thee, even though His face we can't see.

He takes the burdens of our sorrows and replaces them with hope for tomorrow.

Reaching a hand out to someone who has less than you is what God wants us all to do.

God gives love freely to us; He's the One we can truly trust.

Talk to Him like you would a friend - then listen to the message He sends.

Ask for help and He will hear, then look for signs that show He's near.

Call on Him to get you through. One thing's for sure: He is true blue!

When there's darkness and no hope in sight, pray to God for His Heavenly light…

Parents

If I didn't have love from my family, I don't know what would have happened to me.

They cared enough to check out my friends. If they were bad, I couldn't hang around them.

They made sure they had all the numbers where I would be - and would call periodically.

If I was out past nine o'clock, my mom would be up and down the block.

We had things to do around the house; we couldn't just sit and be a mouse.

So we never had to be told what to do - they made rules we had to follow through.

We would get grounded if we did something wrong. That was to help make us strong.

If we had homework to do that night, they would always check to see if it was right.

We weren't allowed to go out and play until all our work was done for that day.

We couldn't eat 'til we were all there; this was our time for the family to share.

They taught us to respect everyone we knew, and by doing so, people will always respect you, too.

They taught us to be kind and to share our things; we learned real early what caring really means.

These are people I want to grow up to be, so I can teach my kids what they taught me.

A Story of Hate, Love, and Faith

As a Teenager

This period of my life is when I was a teenager. It wasn't all fun - that's for sure. I had two different sets of friends I hung out with, but we still all had common interests.

Some of my friends just acted tough, but underneath they were like the rest of us.

Some were square, and if we wanted them to skip with us, they wouldn't dare because they were too scared.

People who were square were called 'socials' in those days. I didn't care; they were still my friends anyways.

My other friends were so-called 'outcasts' - only because they acted up in class.

Some of my friends were judged, of course, just because of the clothes they wore.

Sometimes my grades showed I was slipping because a lot of times we had tests the days I was skipping.

Then I started smoking because it was cool; we'd all meet to smoke before school.

I'd wear a little makeup at first; then I got bolder, so I put more on to look older.

I'd hand out at my girlfriend's house on the weekends; there weren't any grownups around - just friends.

I'd get into it with my mom a lot. She'd think I was getting into trouble, and I'd tell her, "I'm not".

I'd fix my hair the best I could, and some of my friends would call me Phyllis Diller.

Sometimes I'd lie and sneak out, too. When I got home, I was afraid of what they might do.

I'd wear guys' clothes to be discreet so no one could tell I was a girl when I walked the streets.

I'd skip school sometimes, too, just to be with my friends all afternoon.

Dying your hair was the "in thing" to do, so I dyed my hair blonde, too.

I was a leader - not a follower - so I always told them, "I'm not going to mess myself up because of you".

Some of my friends sniffed glue, too. They did some crazy things I couldn't do.

I was always straight, but they didn't care because they knew I didn't like it - and I wouldn't dare.

I didn't want to do drugs nor drink; I cared too much for myself...I think.

Everyone knew they couldn't influence me, so after a while, they'd give up on me.

They accepted me anyway - and I'm still close to a lot of them, even today.

I wanted to grow up real fast, but believe me: If I had to do it all over again, I'd make it last...

A Story of Hate, Love, and Faith

Christmas

Around Christmastime, we'd all go with mom to pick out a tree.
Then we'd take it home for dad to see and decorated it so pretty.
Mom and dad would put lights outside to make the house glow.
It was so beautiful against the snow.
We'd make all kinds of cookies and cut-outs, too; we ate half of
them before we were through.
We decorated them to look nice; our favorite cookies were
Allspice.
We'd save all the money we had, just to buy gifts for mom and
dad.
All of our relatives would come for dinner; we had good times
all through the Winter.
We'd leave milk and cookies out for Santa to eat, then listen at
the window to hear Santa's feet.
We were too excited to sleep Christmas Eve, so we'd creep down
the stairs to see what Santa would leave.
Christmas morning, we couldn't wait - so a lot of noise we would
make.
Mom and dad would get up then come downstairs. Mom would
sit on the couch and dad in his chair.
Our eyes would get big when they'd call our names; no one got
more than the other - we all got the same.
Without a doubt, this is what Christmas is all about…

Darlene S. Watson

Shield

It was lonely - just me and my shield. All good feelings I couldn't yield.

I'd take my shield wherever I'd go so my feelings I didn't have to show.

I didn't like to feel mushy inside; all those feelings I wanted to hide.

I couldn't handle the emotions stirring in me, so I hid them inside so no one could see.

I was scared to let go; love (for me) was hard to show.

I always end up feeling uptight; letting myself go just didn't feel right.

When I felt like I was falling apart, my shield would go up to protect my heart.

I tried to expose myself for who I was, but my protective shield would not budge.

When someone got close, my shield knew what to do. Little by little, my loneliness grew.

My shield made me feel alone and empty a lot. The more it went up, the harder it got.

It was easy for me to give in to my shield that came from within.

I was afraid to let myself feel…that's why I hid behind my shield.

A Story of Hate, Love, and Faith

Betrayed

He always stated what he did for us. He's one person I couldn't trust.

I couldn't stand it when he would yell; when he went to work, all was well.

He was weak. My mom was strong. According to him, she was always wrong.

He talked to my mom like she was dirt; cruel and mean words he would blurt.

In front of people that were around, he would always put her down.

Mom couldn't please him no matter what she did - and took a lot because we weren't his kids.

He didn't talk to her much at all; when he was working, he had a ball.

I can remember my mom happy and free. That all stopped when he tried to mess with me.

I lost my mom after that…he came between us - and that's a fact!

My mom was bowling when he came home and tried to take me to the basement when I was alone.

I pushed him away and ran outside; I went to a friend so I could hide.

I couldn't stop crying 'cause he scared me so. How to tell mom? I didn't know.

I went out and got drunk that night. I sure was a pretty sight.

When I got home, mom was there. She was mad, but I didn't care.

I was still shook up from that afternoon, so I took her upstairs to talk in her room.

I was telling her what he did to me; she didn't believe me - I could see.

Then I told her what sis said and how he'd be kneeling beside my bed.
After that, she fell apart. I blamed myself for breaking her heart.
All because of his lust, he betrayed both of us.

A Story of Hate, Love, and Faith

Me and Her

I stayed up rubbing her head and listened to all the things she said.

She told me everything you could think of. She is my mom who I truly love.

She said things I knew nothing about. She needed me to listen so she could get it out.

When the kids would go out and play, by her side I'd always stay.

She talked to me when I was there; private things she would share.

This was hard for me to take; her pain and sadness I couldn't shake.

I worried about her day and night - and told myself I'd make everything alright.

When I took care of her, I felt grown and took her pain on as my own.

When she hurt, I hurt, too. There wasn't anything for her I wouldn't do.

No matter what, I'd get out of bed when she would call me to rub her head.

It was hard to stay awake, but I forced myself for her sake.

Inside, I would feel really bad because I couldn't bear to see my mom sad.

She would have felt bad if she had known that I put her needs before my own.

We could always relate to each other. I cherish this person who is my mother.

Darlene S. Watson

Mad Hatter

I hated him! Yes, I did! Because of the mean things he did to me when I was a kid.

He pretended to love us a lot; pleasure from hurting us is what he got!

He got a thrill fooling them all and twisted around the things we saw.

I went to the trailer late at night. When I got close, I could hear a fight.

I opened the door and walked in on him; the room wasn't bright, but real dim.

There was blood everywhere - not just on her face, but in her hair.

I liked the lady because I saw her before. He would say she was a no-good whore.

He killed that lady right before my eyes! All that rang in my ears were her cries.

He was enraged and yelling at me. "You're always around spying on me!

"You better not tell, if you know what's good for you. Don't forget: I'm around to pounce on you.

I'll fix it so you'll never tell. I'll make it so you burn in Hell!"

Grandma came looking for me. She found Debbie behind the tree.

Uncle Don came then, just in time to cover up Mad Hatter's crime.

Grandma didn't know what went on - until she saw the lady being buried by Uncle Don.

We helped grandma with our grip; we were told to button our lip.

"Don't tell a soul what you saw. He'll get Whoopy most of all."

Grandma couldn't walk very well...just forget what you saw.

A Story of Hate, Love, and Faith

Control

Moving back and forth with this thing; sleepy eyes this would bring.

He didn't know I was hiding there. I could see Debbie's blank stare.

It was a chain with a ball on the end; doing this to Debbie was Uncle Ben.

My heart was pounding because I knew something was wrong; it wasn't a short chain, but real long.

It sparkled bright in the light. You could see Debbie wasn't looking right.

Debbie's eyes followed the chain. More control he would gain.

"You're under my command to help me whenever you can.

This is a secret between me and you - all the things I'll have you do."

She was nodding her head to all he said.

"You're my little helper. Yes, you are! You can't even tell your sister Dar."

Tick, tock - the time was one. This is why Debbie wasn't having fun.

It was the same time he did this with her; over and over - he had to make sure.

"By the snap of my fingers, you'll do as I say. Not just at night, but in the day."

I got up each time he'd take her; I was alert - that's for sure!

He would have her do horrible things when she was under his spell - not even Pat I would tell.

He didn't like it when I was there. He'd get mad when I'd break Debbie's stare.

It made me sick what he'd make her do. She'd lose her mind if she ever knew.

I didn't like the way he'd make her - when she would stare, I would shake her.

Whenever she was around him, she looked like that. He controlled her mind - and that's a fact!

A Story of Hate, Love, and Faith

Play Along

They did ceremonies to make it seem real. They did them a lot, so it wasn't a big deal.

I was whispering to Pat, "Don't take their pills. Just pretend to lay real still.

Just pretend you're asleep like I did, and don't be afraid when they close the lid."

I'm glad I didn't take that pill. I helped Pat lay real still.

"They won't keep you long in there. They like doing this just to scare."

I didn't take their pill because I knew what they were going to put Pat through.

I had to be alert to help Pat through because they did this to me, too.

I tried to explain to him the best I could and asked him if he understood.

He looked up at me with his eyes and asked me if he was going to die.

I said, "No. You'll just look like you are because they will only go so far."

We called him the enemy - Pat and I - and when he was around, we'd play 'I Spy'.

Because we knew the enemy could hurt, we had a signal to be alert.

We didn't want to be out of each other's sight when the enemy was out, so we'd go to our secret place he knew nothing about.

We had a signal we told each other: Whenever one of us was by ourselves, take cover!

Go to our secret place as fast as you can. We'll be safe there from this evil man.

We loved this place that no one knew; a lot of times, it was just us two.

We didn't take Debbie because she would tell the enemy who had her under his spell.

When she was fine, we'd take her there. She acted like us without her stare…

A Story of Hate, Love, and Faith

Pat

This was the day that Pat was buried alive. I was scared he wouldn't survive.

Pat's arm was dangling down as they laid him in the ground.

When they threw the dirt, it covered all of Pat's shirt.

When the dirt was thrown, Uncle Ben held us tight. We struggled to get free with all our might.

He wasn't moving, but laid real still - after they gave him one of their pills.

It was out in the woods where this took place. I didn't take their pill…just in case.

Pat was crying and trying to get out. He left him there to rot.

We were crying so hard; we fell in a heap. He buried Pat alive! What a creep!

They told us it was just a game. It was real just the same.

Pat was laying there like he was asleep; he wouldn't move or make a peep.

They wanted us to see Pat's body lying dead - all because I wasn't in my bed.

Me and Debbie cried and cried because our little brother had just died.

Pat couldn't take it. I heard his screams. This was real and not a dream.

"Where is he? Where is he?" I screamed out loud! I would get him back - I vowed!

"Please! Take me instead! I was the one who was out of bed. I won't tell, honest I won't. Don't take Pat! Please, don't!"

"Whoopy got you into this mess. Now let's see if she really cares less."

They did this on purpose so he would learn that what they did wasn't our concern.

There was a spot they used a lot. Buried alive is what we got.

They used Pat as a bribe…we had to search for him if we wanted to see him alive.

To find Pat, we had to dig in the dirt. After a while, our arms would hurt.

Pat's screams rang in my head. If we can't find him, he'll be dead! I worried about Pat and Debbie. I knew they couldn't take it as much as I.

A lot of times, I took their place for all the things they couldn't face.

I took a lot from Uncle Ben because I couldn't see them tortured even then...

A Story of Hate, Love, and Faith

Got Caught

He saw me spying on him one night. I took off full of fright.

He kicked me like a dog because he knew what I saw.

He kicked dogs like he kicked me; these were some of the things I would see.

In the kitchen, he slapped my face. Back and forth, he would pace.

I stood there and wouldn't cry. I wished he would die!

He was yelling, "You were out spying!" I told him I wasn't…but I was lying.

He pushed me hard and I fell to the floor. When he was done, I was real sore (mad).

I didn't flinch when he kicked me there - and showed him I didn't care.

That made him madder, so he kicked me harder and was ranting even louder.

I was mad - I'll tell you that! But I'd find a way to get him back.

I laid there not feeling a thing. She took over: Her name is Darlene.

After she left, I felt the pain she shielded from me. She is also a part of me.

She holds all my rage and anger, too. Don't mess with me - I'm telling you!

I wasn't afraid to tell on him; Don't you see? Because I had my shield to protect me.

I have this feeling I can't explain. All I know, powerful strength I gain.

My shield is made of strong steel; it comes up so I can't feel.

Darlene came out full of rage, but I don't know at what age.

People wouldn't know by looking at me that I have a shield that protects all of me.

All the energy, my shield used - just so I wouldn't feel my abuse.

He brought my shield out the first time I was ripped apart.

Darlene S. Watson

Halloween

Halloween night, I was full of fright. Everything was black and hidden in the night.

Someone grabbed my hand and pulled me inside. It was so dark, there was no place to hide.

A lot of ugly faces coming at me; I shut my eyes so I couldn't see.

A flash of light to distort their looks...hanging skeletons on hooks.

A real House of Horrors with doors everywhere; they took us there just to scare.

Weird sounds of voices all around; no one knew I could be found.

I was too scared, so I stood real still. There was someone standing at the window sill.

She came towards me dressed in black. I could hear a train coming down the track.

Her face was ugly, her chin was long; I want out of there, where I didn't belong.

With a hat on her head and long black hair, her high-pitched voice gave me a scare.

I couldn't move; I was too much in fright. All I could see was the witch in sight.

I was petrified - that's for sure! Some things I remember; the rest is a blur.

I don't like Halloween costumes still today because of that night. To scare kids to death just wasn't right...

A Story of Hate, Love, and Faith

Masks

They dug a hole that wasn't too deep and put Pat in it so he could sleep.

When I saw them put him there, I started to weep. "Leave him alone, you creep!"

"We'll play a game so you won't know each other - and wear a mask undercover.

"Put this on over your face." I didn't want to; my heart would race.

They were scary and spooky, too. They'd make us wear them - just us two.

My head hurt so bad wearing it; pounding inside I would get.

It wasn't so bad looking at it…I just didn't want to wear it.

I got used to the way it looked, and when I'd wear it, I shook.

My head would pound putting it on. He would make me: His name is Don.

This was one of his pranks he'd play. "This is all in fun", he would say.

He'd do things with his dad that were really bad.

He hit me so I'd fall down, then they put me in the ground.

When I looked up, I saw the face with those eyes because he was wearing a disguise.

That mask he had on scared me so. After seeing that I didn't know.

"Who do you think is behind the mask?" they'd ask, then take them off after their task.

They didn't care if we knew them or not because they would do these things a lot.

The skeleton head was on Don.

Those eyes were in someone's head…who was dead.

Darlene S. Watson

When I Was Thirteen

I cried most of my teenage years. All I can remember were the tears.

My mom and dad treated me mean. All I wanted was to get out of that scene.

No love lost there; they just plain didn't care.

Because of my dad's lust, he broke my heart and my trust.

I took the blame on what he did; I felt shame when I was a kid.

I had no worth or value that I could see, and this is how I thought of me.

My stepdad wanted me in bed. He didn't want my mom; he wanted me instead.

There was no peace in our house to speak of - and no love that I knew of.

She caught him with me when I was just thirteen.

She stayed with him over me; he was happy, I could see. He always messed with me.

I was afraid to be alone when she wasn't home.

I was empty inside...all my feelings I wanted to hide.

I hurt so bad inside of me; I just wanted to be loved, I believe.

I hated myself for how I felt; I needed a release to get it out.

I was shy and timid, too. I didn't have anyone to talk to.

I dealt with my pain the only way I knew how, and hating myself brought this about.

All they did was fight over me. She was jealous - I could see.

When I was fifteen, I wanted a baby...for someone to love and love me, too.

I got involved with a guy I knew. He was bad for me, too!

He'd beat me bad all the time - for no reason or rhyme.

A Story of Hate, Love, and Faith

Shame

I met this guy when I was fifteen. I found out he was real mean.
I fell in love, too. His anger grew.
He would beat me up in front of his friends. I just took it 'til it would end.
He took drugs and drank, too; this is all he would do.
He pressured me for sex…I gave in. I cried and cried because I had sinned.
I got pregnant when I was eighteen. By then, I thought he loved me.
I married him, too. He'd beat me when nobody knew.
When our son was six months old, he beat him, too.
I was in shock, too!
I was too scared to call the police on him; he would never do that again.
I stayed up with him all night, just to make sure he was alright.
He'd rape me over and over whenever I said "NO!" How I made it, I don't know.
I wanted to get away from him. My fear was sinking in.
He would never leave me; I knew I wouldn't be free.
I cried to God to get me out of this mess. When he died, I was blessed.
I don't regret that I felt this way. I have a good life since that day.
Over his grave, I said to him that no man would ever hurt me like that again.
I learned that my home life caused me to have no self-worth, so I felt I deserved what he did to me.
Two people who said they loved me broke my heart and used and abused me.
I made it because God was there; He made me strong from all the things I couldn't bear.
Today, I am healthy and whole. God has healed my soul! Praise the LORD!!!

Darlene S. Watson

A House Divided

It was hard to grasp the things I saw. I couldn't stand the fighting most of all.

I saw them drunk an awful lot; the more they drank, the worse it got.

He would beat my mom up really bad. I didn't like my stepdad.

After being up half the night listening to them fight, I'd go to school always uptight.

There were three of us mom had before; then she married again - and had three more.

Us three took care of the younger three, just so they could do what they pleased.

There was a lot of responsibility we had to endure. It was Hell - that's for sure!

She spent a lot of time arguing with dad, and this made us all very sad.

Then she'd go in her room and shut the door…and shut us out even more.

We never had any examples of love growing up to know, so that's why it's hard for us to show.

We were always separated from those three. We were the stepkids…they were family.

We weren't allowed to get ahead because we had to deal with their problems instead.

While we were taking care of grownup things our mother should have done, they were allowed to have all the fun.

A lot of the things mom didn't want them to know, so her good side she would show.

We knew her one way and they knew her another; that's because she always treated them like a mother.

With us, it was always telling us what to do - and if we didn't, it was shame on you.

There was never any peace to speak of, and never showing us any kind of love.

A Story of Hate, Love, and Faith

There was always tension in the air; that's why I always hated being there.

Mom was always in depression - I could always tell by her expressions.

She would stay in bed day after day; I used to wish it would all go away.

I was depressed and lonely, too. I just didn't know what to do.

I was mad a lot because she was always sick. If I could choose, she wouldn't be the mother I would pick.

She slept all day and partied all night. She didn't care if we were alright.

She put herself first and us last, just so she could have a blast...

Darlene S. Watson

My Opinion

Our family has always gone their own way and for some, that was OK.

Now that there is a problem, no one wants to say; so everyone's solution is to just stay away.

There has been a lot of deception, and this has caused misconception.

If I have a problem with another, I take it to them - not my mother.

I take each one on how they treat me, and that's the way I'm always going to be.

I'm responsible for the things I say and do. If you ask what I think, I'm going to tell you.

I can't answer for what other people do, so don't expect me to.

I was always honest to each one of you. You took it out on me, not caring if it was true.

I'm well aware how everyone feels about me, so no matter what I do, you'll never see.

After all I've been through, everybody is the same; instead of looking at yourselves, I take the blame.

There are always two sides to a story, and if no one knows that - I feel sorry.

I'm not involved in this mess; to be honest, I couldn't care less.

I have always been for my family, but it takes more than just me.

This family has been this way for as long as I can remember, and it involves every member.

The way everybody has acted is quite clear that the only one you'll listen to is mother dear.

I can't believe that people don't cherish today, because tomorrow we could all be taken away.

God blessed me to live my life with peace and love - not chaos and strife.

I thought when I came close to death you would all see that there is nothing more important than family.

A Story of Hate, Love, and Faith

I love each and every one of you, I do know; and that's why it's easy for me to show.

You shut me out and hurt my heart. If that's how you feel, we can stay apart.

I can't have stress from all this mess, and if there is - you'll see me less and less.

Darlene S. Watson

How I Felt

I was numb…without any pain. It was unbearable just the same.

They'd holler a lot when I was around. Half the time, I couldn't touch ground.

There was stress in our house; I would hide like a mouse.

There was no peace to speak of. There were no signs of love.

I didn't like being there as a kid. I hated everything they did.

They would holler most of the time; most of the days, I wasn't fine.

I was sick most of the time. I just wasn't fine.

I couldn't cope (most of all). When they went out, they had a ball.

They'd leave us alone a lot. Bad headaches are what I got.

I would shake inside - they would hide their good side.

Mom wasn't around very much. She never had a loving touch.

The look she gave me scared me a lot; a nervous stomach is what I got.

I was afraid of her…she could hurt.

I was afraid of her, that's for sure. Most of the time, I lived in a blur.

She didn't care that I wanted to die; all I did was cry and cry.

She spent a lot of time arguing with dad. This made us all very sad.

We never had any examples of love growing up to know, so that's why it's hard for us to show.

There was three of us mom had before, then she married and had three more!

Us three took care of the younger three, just so they could do as they please.

She'd go in to her room and shut the door, and shut us out even more.

While we were taking care of grownup things our mother should have done, they were allowed to have all the fun.

She'd put her needs before us; we hardly saw her when she was with stepdad.

Mom took it out on us because we were in the way of her and stepdad.

If things went wrong with her and dad, she'd make us feel like we were bad.

She wanted us to be real quiet when he was around; she worshipped the ground he walked on.

When he'd be mad because things weren't done, she punished us from having any fun.

When they first got together and they had a baby, they only took him and left the rest of us.

They wanted a family - and us out of the way. Mom still treats us that way today.

Mom and dad never treated us with respect. We weren't his kids - what do you expect?

Mom was different with us when she had kids from her husband (stepdad).

She hated Debbie and us, too. When she'd say, "I'll give you kids away", that was my clue.

He always tells us what he did for us; he hasn't changed - he still does.

They thought more of Katie and Sally - and love for them was easy to show.

When they came along, there was rivalry. We never felt like a family.

Unconditional love is what they had; that's because they were their real mom and dad.

We had to make it any way we could; they never gave us support the way parents should.

Our relationship with mom ended when she had the other three. Her and dad and them were now a family.

We didn't have our own dad - and we lost her, too. Us three stuck together like glue.

We weren't allowed to go out and play. We had to do mom's work that day.

Katie and Sally were allowed to come and go. When we wanted to do something, we were always told "NO!"

They made us feel like we were a burden to them - and complain about the money they'd spend.

Dad would boast about how he took us in; not once, but over and over again.

He acted like he did us a favor. We always heard it sooner or later.

My mom had us all, but she didn't care about us. She cared more for the kids she had with stepdad.

If we had to have our teeth done, they'd throw that up, too; and tell us how much money they had to "spend on you".

They never encouraged us to be our best in anything we wanted to do. They always threw up to us, "We could have a lot if it wasn't for you."

A Story of Hate, Love, and Faith

Devil in Disguise

All your anger and jealousy you want to hide, just so we can be fooled by your good side.

You're so phony, you often slip. When you're mad, you let it rip.

You don't care whose feelings you hurt; that's why I'm always alert.

You lie only to suit you, and don't even care if it's true.

You do a lot undercover; after all, you are my mother.

But I know you better than you think I do - and one thing I know: You're not true blue.

You play games because you think you're smart, but all you're doing is tearing your family apart.

One by one, you take us aside - because if we were all together, we'd know you lied.

You have a side I've always seen. It wasn't nice…it was always mean.

I never seen a mother like you - one who deliberately hurts her kids like you do.

When you're nice, I'm on my guard. Trusting you is very hard.

You twist and turn the things you do, just so everyone will look bad - except you.

You pick and choose who you love, because in your mind, we're not good enough.

Lies and deceit come out when you speak. The ones who listen are the ones who are weak.

The weak ones, you like to snare - because if they wanted to question you, they wouldn't dare.

Whatever you give out will come back to you, so I would be careful…if I were you - and you're the only one who knows what you do.

I'm always on my toes when I'm around you - because I never know what you'll do.

Because of the things you say and the way you act, I know you talk behind my back.

Without a doubt, I'm very aware that you just don't care.

You don't want love; you want a fight. That's because you walk in darkness and not the light.

You push everybody away that loves you, then blame them for the things you do.

Put the blame where it belongs, and accept the things you do wrong.

You have your family you had from stepdad, so you don't care about the rest of us...

A Story of Hate, Love, and Faith

Whose Side Are You On?

The times I cried and cried were because I knew she lied.

All the secrets she wants to hide tells me she was on their side.

Good and bad she can be; when she's bad, she turns on me.

She's as clever as she can be; that's why she was always my adversary.

I wasn't one of them. That was interesting, too. That was also another clue.

She treated me like an enemy. She also tried to get rid of me.

Some part of me has always known that one day I would stand alone.

She was cold-blooded even then; she took sides with her brother, Ben.

I ranted and raged about her, too, because I knew she was true blue.

When the truth comes out, she'll deny it - without a doubt.

It wasn't easy to accept that all they wanted was to see me dead.

Cat and mouse I have to play - and watch what I say.

She is devious I well know; she can fool you because it doesn't show.

I know the faces and the names; they were strangers - or so she claims.

She doesn't like to hear what her family did to me; she just wants me to let things be.

There is no change since the flashbacks hit - that I can see. She still puts her family before me.

Even though I know the faces, she tries to change the scenes and the places.

A lot of them were family members. She hates me...because I remember.

She is loyal to her family - where I'm concerned. Through all of this, I have learned.

If seeing me out of my mind for almost a year from their torture and abuse, and that didn't affect her...then what's the use?

I accept the fact she'll never love me - not as much as her family. Not to fear, because God is always near. He will help me go up against Mother Dear...

A Story of Hate, Love, and Faith

Stepdad

He'd sneak in my room to read my diary. He was always nosy when it came to me.

Then he started coming in my room late at night. The things he was doing to me wasn't right.

He'd always kiss me on the mouth - and French kiss me. Would you believe?

He'd tell me lies about my mother and tell me she'd find no other.

He always put her down and never said anything nice about her when I was around.

He was always spying on me. When he was around, I never had peace. When he went to work, what a relief!

I shook all the time I was home because I didn't want us to be alone.

He'd pit my mom against me, too. There were all kinds of things he loved to do.

He loved to see her jealousy; that's why he built me up, you see?

He got a kick out of seeing hurt; cruel and mean words he'd blurt.

When my mom caught him in my room next to me, she was in shock I could see.

After that, nothing between us was the same; instead of getting rid of him, I took the blame.

He held things over my head, too. He never voiced it, but somehow I always knew.

He also knew his secrets were safe with me because I couldn't hurt my family.

Mom and him fought a lot over me, and that hurt me deeply.

I was always their go-between; both of them treated me mean.

I never understood why she took his side, and when she did, I cried and cried.

I ran away a few times because they treated me so bad - all because of a man I called 'dad'.

Everything he stands for I despise; a nice man he wears in disguise.

There's no excuse for what he put me through. I still carry scars from that - I tell you!

He loved it when she went against me, and the message he got was he could do what he pleased.

He acted like he cared about me, but in reality, he was a phony.

She'd accuse me of wanting him, too. I was only a kid! What could I do?

For years, him and her made me feel dirty; they made me think that I wasn't worthy.

He used me and abused me and broke my heart. I didn't trust him from the start!

I stayed around because I wanted a family and overlooked the pain they caused me.

You both made me pay because of your sickness. The feelings I have for you now are less and less.

A thousand years, I'll cry for me because neither one of you ever loved me...and now, I'm FREE!

A Story of Hate, Love, and Faith

Out of Touch

Every time someone hurt me, little by little it chipped away my true being, so all the bad memories were what I was feeling.

When you're a victim as a child, pain inside is what drives us wild.

Acting out is what we do best. The pain inside won't give us any rest.

When pain hangs around like an old shoe, we're so tore up, we don't know what to do.

Layers and layers of defenses we wear; our true self we can't even bear.

Denial is one that is living a lie and doesn't like to hear good-bye.

Fantasy is another that takes us to another place, for all the things we couldn't face.

Blame is one that covers the mess and makes us feel less and less.

Face to face, I want to see how this happened and how to break free.

It's hard at first to begin because all of these things are within.

This is a step that I had to take in order for me to clean my slate.

They've been a part of me for so long, I felt they were there to make me strong - but boy, was I wrong!

It took a while to confront each one, and when they didn't come back, I knew I had won.

Now I know when my insides feel yuck, those feelings creep in to keep me stuck.

I tell myself that they no longer exist for me, and when I confront them, I feel free.

Now that I have no layers to shed, I no longer feel pain; just peace instead.

I see myself in a new light, and that's because I put up a fight.

I didn't want the past to hinder me any longer; believe me - I'm much stronger!

There were times I didn't know what to do, then God came to help me through.

When I forgave the ones who hurt me in the past, my healing came very fast.

Forgiving them set me free to know myself as God knows me...

A Story of Hate, Love, and Faith

Uptight

I couldn't relax when he was around. I'd go to my room and not make a sound.

He was always spying on me; he would even read my diary.

In my room he would stay. He would think it was OK.

He'd say things to me in front of my mom that weren't right; those were the times I wish I was out of sight.

He'd lift me up and put her down. He'd do it a lot when I was around.

He'd French Kiss me, too. I didn't know what to do.

He had lust for me then; it's always been.

He broke my heart when he ripped me apart.

I was young and in my prime. He was after me all the time.

Because of his lust, he is one person I couldn't trust.

I couldn't relax when he was home. "Please", I prayed, "leave me alone!"

I shed a lot of tears for me just because he wouldn't let me be.

My mom didn't stand up for me and never took me out of that scene.

She turned on me time and time again. I couldn't trust her even then.

She used to accuse me of wanting him, too. I was just a kid: What could I do?

He betrayed me and broke my heart. I loved him from the start.

I was three when I first met him. I liked him right away. I never knew it would turn out this way.

I loved him like a dad. He made me very sad.

I trusted him to take care of me and love me, too; it was bad what he would do.

I was tense when he was home. He would kiss me whenever we were alone.

I told on him when I was a kid. I hated him…I really did.

They'd fight over me when they were drunk. My heart just sunk in despair; what they said, I couldn't bear.

She was always mad at me for what he did; she turned on me when I was a kid.

I needed someone to help me cope. I didn't feel any hope.

No one understands what I went through. I think they believe it's not true.

He's gone now. I forgave him and let it go. I got healed in my soul.

A Story of Hate, Love, and Faith

Computer

Our minds are computers that store all our information and can call up things on any given situation.

It records everything we've ever been through and gives us directions on what to do.

Our computer we can trust because the information we put in is a part of us.

Our computer doesn't forget - even the things we can't accept.

Our computer is so cunning that even though we shut it off, it's still running.

We have a memory bank that never stops, and if we're not ready, it automatically goes to block.

All computers have a name. The most popular ones are called pain.

We're programming it all the time; another name for it is our mind.

What's great is that we all have one of our own. How you use yours, nobody knows.

To get into mine, you have to put Dar. If you put the wrong code in, you won't get too far.

We all have a codename we go by; all it is is you and I.

Some of us use our computer every day so we can be better that way.

Our computer gives us a printout to work out when we're down and keeps us busy 'til we come around.

If we're not strong enough to view a situation, our computer will often deny access to any information.

Sometimes we think we're ready to begin, but our computer knows better and won't let anything in.

We can only handle bad memories a little at a time. If we remember too much at once, we would lose our minds!

Our computer protects our soul from all the traumas we went through before.

Sometimes our computer gets overloaded with information, so sometimes it will take a vacation.

That's when you take a break - for your own sake.

Our computer will only do what we tell it to do, so we're always safe if we want to skip a situation that we don't want to view.

We need our computer throughout our whole life because without a mind, we couldn't survive...

A Story of Hate, Love, and Faith

Listen Up!

Hate and death are the masks they wear; pain inside too much to bear.

Kids in gangs with a code of their own; no place to call 'Home Sweet Home'.

No hope. No dreams. Nowhere to turn. Pain so deep, their only way out is a deep, deep sleep.

Drugs and guns made them brave, taking them to an early grave.

Mother and fathers down on their luck, looking to score to make a buck.

Kids growing up before their time, with no hope - turning to crime.

Kill or be killed is all they know; greed and hate told them so.

Years of neglect and abuse made them think, "What's the use?"

A hug…a touch doesn't cost a dime. We're too busy to take the time.

People in a big house with plenty to eat have no thought of the kids in the street.

How easy we forget - when we're doing so well - that life for some is a living Hell.

Gone are the days of helping each other; now all we hear is brother killing brother!

Drugs and guns are everywhere, only because no one cares.

Some never had a chance from day one; the answer to their problems was a gun.

Guns are their power and their friend; death won out in the end.

If we don't do something to end the bloodshed, more and more kids will be dead.

Love is the power to end all this hate.

We've got to come together…before it's too late.

Darlene S. Watson

Tolerance

Acceptance comes when we understand that we all come from God's plan.

If we could see the good we all possess, we would see faults less and less.

Our tolerance is put to a test so we can see that no one is any better than you or me.

The lessons we learn are pain in disguise; we wouldn't change otherwise.

Right a wrong that has been done so we don't carry it the next day - if we need to say I'm sorry, do it right away!

Set an example with good cheer for all the ones that are close and dear.

Extend your heart and your hand, but most of all - try and understand.

When someone is sad and down, a smile…a touch can bring 'em around.

Everyone has their own pain to bear, and it hurts more when no one's there.

We need to remember that we've been in pain, too; and with the help from a loved one, we made it through.

Every one of us has faults - we know. When we focus on them, there's no room to grow.

A smile here and there is a good place to start; treat each other with an open heart.

Some people don't know how to reach out; showing we care tells them that they count.

Put yourself in their place and think twice. It only takes a minute to be nice.

Love can mend and repair when times are dark and we're in despair.

So, take time out of your busy day to be kind along the way…

A Story of Hate, Love, and Faith

Actions Speak Louder Than Words

If you say "I love you" and get their trust, then go to someone else - not caring whose heart we crushed.

If we listen to a friend who confides in us, then go tell someone else all they had to say.

If someone asks you if they look alright, then you make fun of them when they're out of your sight.

Even when you take things from your job and it doesn't belong to you, believe it or not: That's stealing, too.

When you tell a fib and you say it's a 'White Lie', no it's not: It's a lie in disguise.

When you talk about people behind their back, it's because we don't like to hear facts.

Men pushing women around out of their anger, just because they don't like the change in her.

Putting someone down because we had a bad day is no excuse; no one deserves verbal abuse.

If kids see their parents physically fighting and don't understand, they'll grow up thinking they can raise their hand.

When you blow up over the littlest things, you're letting them know that you're out of control.

Punishing someone who you love by not talking to them, "I'm not important" is the message you send.

When you're in a relationship with nothing but abuse around, kids in families like that always put themselves down.

If abuse is all we know, it's because parents showed us so.

If we showed love in a negative way because that's all we knew, then we would think of it as normal behavior as we grew.

When kids see their parents treating each other with disrespect and they have none, what do you expect?

There are so many different types of abuse that hurt us layer by layer. It carries its mark sooner or later.

We should always make sure our values are intact before we put other people under our attack…

Kids

Kids are what we used to be, so think of them as you and me.

They're so easily influenced by what they see because they copy you and me.

Sometimes the people they love just leave, then they don't know what to believe.

They think it's because of something they've done wrong, so they feel they don't belong.

They feel so insecure about their future, too, and feel that there is no one they can turn to.

Abandonment of any kind leaves a hole in their soul, so throughout their life, they try and fill it up with junk more and more.

Then there are kids who are deceived by people who say they love them, and after a while, they don't know what to believe.

When kids mistrust, it's hard to build them up again, so they go through life having suspicions of everybody in the end.

They easily believe the things you say; if it's not good, they'll remember them always.

People do things to kids because of their own pain. Poor, innocent kids take the blame all the same.

If people don't get help when they know they're out of control, they eventually take it out on kids - as you well know.

When people beat on their kids most of their lives, they damage their souls and make it hard for them to survive.

From then on, their lives are filled with nothing but pain, and spend half their life regaining it again.

It's a shame what kids go through. How they grow up depends on you.

Then there are some kids who never make it at all. Some were killed before they grew tall - and some before they even crawled.

Some people don't think there is anything wrong with them, and by the time they get help, their kids are already dead.

Some people treat their kids with abuse because that's all they're used to.

A lot of parents lost control at times; seeking help will bring you peace of mind.

Kids are keepsakes to love and protect - not to hate. Please get help before it's too late...

Darlene S. Watson

Us Three

When we were young, we loved everyone.

I was curious and talked a lot: I wanted to know what people were about.

We would love to play. A lot of people pushed us away.

We weren't like them - we could see. It was always just us three.

We would laugh a lot and make faces, too; just to cheer us up, that's what we would do.

We had a bond no one could break. We loved each other for our sakes.

If one of us was sad and down, we would laugh 'til we came around.

It was easy to be together. We always felt so much better.

We had no one who really cared about us. Our grandma was the one we could trust.

She would wash our faces and comb our hair; she was the one who was always there.

We'd rub her feet and her legs 'til she was fine. We did this all the time.

She'd buy us donuts once a week. This was our weekly treat.

We loved her the most out of everyone; with her we had so much fun.

She would read the Bible to us each day; that was to keep the evil away.

She'd listen to us three. She'd say, "Hark, hark! Listen to me!"

She would talk to us real nice and sweet; we always sat by her feet.

We would take our naps with her, too. This is what we loved to do.

She would black out a lot, too. We were too young to know what to do.

She loves us - we could tell by what she did, always being good to us kids.

Then we moved and didn't see her much. We all missed her touch.

Patience

We're always in a hurry to get things done, never looking at anyone.

I found out today (while waiting in line) that just looking around brought me peace of mind.

Then I started thinking, "What if they were going through suffering?" No one knew...

When I look at someone and don't even know their name, I still pray for them all the same.

Someone in front of me was in a wheelchair. I felt sad because she was there.

I touched a hand when I needed direction on which to go; she wanted the same! What do you know!

Then I was in the bathroom in the store and who do I see? My sister Susan!

We said our "Hellos" and "Good-byes", seeing her was a nice surprise.

Then I had to exchange my gloves for another pair, and there was a problem - but I didn't care because I was in prayer with God while standing there.

He calmed me down and gave me peace. All through the day, my patience increased.

I felt so good because I enjoyed my day, glad I didn't rush away.

There's a lesson I learned today: When I get impatient, I need to pray because a lot of times, we've all had a bad day.

Patience comes very fast when we are kind, and it will increase over time.

So, as you hurry through your day, remember: Kindness goes a long way!

Little Angels

Kids are what dreams are made of. They're so sweet and easy to love, given to us from God above.

Kids bring joy to our lives and make our lives feel worthwhile.

They lift us up when we've had a bad day, and make all our problems seem far away.

When they take their first step, we feel so proud and keep smiling when they fall down.

When we hear their first word, like mom or dad, our heads swell. We are so proud - you can tell!

When they get hurt, we kiss their boo-boos and tell them we kissed them better - and they believe us, too.

When we boast about our kids to someone else, we're so proud - you can hear in our voice.

Some are so good, they never cry. Then there are some that cry all the time.

Some talk early because they can't wait to get out what they're all about.

They have a language all their own, and a lot of times, they love to talk on the phone.

Their expressions tell us how they feel, and when we tickle them, they squeal.

They love to play patty-cake, and happy sounds they make.

They walk around picking things up as they go, and we try to teach them the word 'no'.

They laugh a lot over the things they see, and run with open arms to you and me.

At bedtime, we read them nursery rhymes just so they'll have peace of mind.

Some don't say anything, but make loud sounds. They even scream out loud.

They love it when we give them a bath, and all their little toys they have to have.

Their skin is so soft and they smell so good; if I could be little again, I would.

They copy us, too, and love to show off what they can do.

We think they're asleep when we're out of sight, but a lot of times they cry and we're up with them half the night.

We try and soothe them so they can sleep - and so can we - but sometimes they're hard to please.

They are demanding and take up a lot of time. We love them so much, we don't mind.

They remind us of the way we used to be, when we see how they love us freely.

We need to always remember this:

Our lives would be a heck of a lot different without our kids…

A Story of Hate, Love, and Faith

Angels

Angels are a gift from God to protect us wherever we trod.

There are some angels we don't see; then there are some angels that are like you and me.

These angels we see are people in disguise. They help us through our earthly lives.

The ones that are invisible to the naked eye are sent from God to be our tour guides.

God sent angels to comfort our fears, and sometimes they even wipe our tears.

Spiritual angels are the lifeline to God to protect us from harm when we get alarmed.

If you're looking for something that is hard to find, ask an angel and you'll find it all the time.

Angels protect us, too, when we're asleep and give us peace - our soul to keep.

They're here to help us find our way, and are here for us as long as we want them to stay.

They're here to comfort us through our trials and tribulations, and to watch for us when we get impatient.

Have you ever felt that someone pulled you back just in the nick of time? That was your angel being so kind.

They flutter around spreading their kindness; even if we don't see them, we feel their closeness.

Some of us know them by their names; others feel them just the same.

They're kind and gentle and smile a lot; they're so happy to help us out.

They're so eager to help us whenever they can; they came from God - and not from man.

God sends them all about because he knows we need them a lot.

Flutter here…flutter there…not to worry! We're always in their care.

Darlene S. Watson

God sends angels to watch over all of us, so through them we feel His love.

He gave us Guardian Angels so we wouldn't be alone; without them, we couldn't do anything on our own.

Spiritual angels and earthly angels have one thing in common: They love everyone around them.

So, little ones - and big ones, too: Don't forget there's an angel out there for you, too, who watches over you!

A Story of Hate, Love, and Faith

Look Around

Life is unfair, we do believe; pain and suffering is all we see.

Fear is taking over all the time, and this is the force that resorts to crime.

Love is hard to express these days. Fear takes its place in all ways.

Without love, we can't cope. Without God, there is no hope.

Our kids are killing each other every day; without our help, it won't go away.

People are homeless with nothing to eat; they need our help to get back on their feet.

If we could see that life is good, then we would help the way we should.

Life is in our hands to do our best. When we do, our minds are at rest.

No one wants to be shut out. When we focus on just the bad things, this is what brings it about.

Love shines through when we give to each other; after all, we are sisters and brothers!

Life has its ups and downs - we all know. Showing love makes us grow.

Love is so profound because it has the power to turn us around.

We need to see what it is we lack so we can bring Salvation back.

When all is lost, just remember that God is the one to whom we must surrender.

We're in this life to do God's work for all mankind; loving each other brings peace of mind.

He is a person, place, or thing; knowing this, our hearts will sing.

When we grow and thrive, we are keeping God alive.

Yes, fear is what keeps us all apart, but showing love warms our heart.

A closed mind cannot change; only an open mind can rearrange.

Love is what we all need to give, so the world will be a better place to live.

Darlene S. Watson

God is with Me

He's the only one who knows what's going on. With Him there is a special bond.

I wasn't really living (so to speak), then I put my life in God's hands my soul to keep.

When I got the news that I had cancer in my breast, I knew whatever the reason, God knew best.

If God says I can bear this, I truly can; this is between God and me - and not man.

I am blessed with this burden I bear, and through it all, God has been there.

He keeps me going day by day; I pray to Him to find my way.

I am blessed with all I have around me, and this is what God really wants me to see.

God opened my eyes so I could see that there are people worse off than me.

To kill the cancer, I have to take chemo; there are many side effects I didn't even know.

I was given only three months to live - according to man; but to see that wasn't God's plan.

I was so scared that I cried and cried. I told God I didn't want to die.

After a while, I felt at ease. I was surrounded in His peace.

The news I heard gave me no hope, but I looked to God to help me cope.

Then the miracle came that gave me a chance. The doctors told me I was candidate for a transplant!

God gave me the strength to endure that, too.

The chemo they gave me made me so sick and out of my head, but I knew without it, I would be dead.

I didn't doubt that I was in God's care; He gave me signs that showed me He was there.

He sent His angels to minister to me; when I felt them, I was so relieved.

A Story of Hate, Love, and Faith

God says when we're weak, we're strong; that's because God's been with us all along.

When fear would come in my mind, He would settle me down until I was fine.

He told me things that let me know He was there, and one of them was how much He cared.

It wasn't my courage - I knew - but God's love that brought me through.

I couldn't have made it, that's for sure! God is the only one who has the cure.

I thank God with all my heart that He had mercy on me, and in my life I want Him to be.

I witnessed what God can do and what He did for me; He can do the same for you if you believe.

He strengthened my belief when He pulled me through. I can say for sure: He is true!

Darlene S. Watson

My Healing

I was cleaning the house one day and on TV were women who had found a lump in their breasts. I didn't know it then, but I was to find one myself. My underarm was all swollen and pinched. I made an appointment to see the doctor. The day I went, I was so lost in thought that when they called my name, I didn't hear at first. I was so glad they called me in because by that time, my mind was working overtime. I had to wait a few more minutes before getting into an examining room.

Finally, she came in and I felt myself relax...a little. She asked how I was doing. I told her, "Fine". I told her the reason I came to see her was because I had a problem with my arm and discovered a lump in my breast, too. She tells me to lift my arm up so she could get a better look. She checks my arm and feels around the area that was swollen. Then she takes her fingers and examines the lump. After she was finished, she asked me how long had I known about the lump. I told her about a week. I told her that the problem I was having with my arm caused me to discover the lump. She told me that she was going to try to aspirate it with a needle. She told me to just lie still and not to worry; that it wouldn't hurt.

She had one of her assistants come in to help her. When she was done, she told me that nothing came out, so she was going to refer me to a surgeon right away. I got alarmed after hearing that. I asked her if she thought something was wrong, and she replied, "I just want to make sure it is taken care of. The surgeon will know more about it than I do at this point."

A Story of Hate, Love, and Faith

I'm trying to stay calm, hoping it wasn't too serious - and praying that everything would be alright. She told me she wanted to see me again after my visit with the surgeon. As I left her office, fear took over. I thought, "If a surgeon had to see me, maybe it was serious after all…"

I returned home full of fear. I started to pray to God to take my fear away. After a while, the fear left me. I thought about everything the doctor did and called my mom. I told her what the doctor said and that I would have to see a surgeon. She gave me encouragement. I hung up the phone and tried to rest.

The next few weeks were a blur. I went from fear to outright terror. I kept praying to God, and He kept giving me peace.

The day came when I went to see the surgeon. He aspirated the lump, too - but nothing came out. By that time, I was crying and showed him my armpit. He didn't say anything about it. I left his office the same way I went in. There was no more information than before.

In the meantime, I had an appointment with my D.O. I showed him my underarm and he couldn't believe it. He is the one who brought up a biopsy. He was surprised the surgeon didn't mention it. He told me to get a biopsy right away. I couldn't believe that five months had gone by…and no biopsy. After I left his office, I called the surgeon and told him what the doctor said. He agreed…FINALLY.

On February 8th, my son and I arrived at the hospital. I had to go to Admitting to fill out the necessary papers for surgery. I could see my son was nervous. I know it was hard for him - not knowing what would happen. After the papers were signed, they came and took me to get prepped for surgery. My son sat and talked to me until they came to wheel me away to the operating room. I felt bad for him waiting out there by himself. I told him not to worry; that it shouldn't take long.

I remember being in a daze sitting there with my son, still groggy from surgery. When I see the doctor walk towards me and pull up a chair, I knew something was wrong. He takes my hands, puts his head down, and says, "I'm sorry to tell you: The biopsy showed an advanced stage of cancer." I grabbed both of his hands and just bawled. I looked over at my son, and he was crying and shaking his head back and forth as the doctor was talking. At that point, I couldn't grasp anything he was saying.

The hospital is also where I worked, so I had my son go and get my girlfriend I worked with to come and sit with me. I have no idea what I said to her when she sat down. I told her what the doctor said - and don't recall anything after that.

I do remember thinking (after I settled down) that God brought Job of the Bible to my mind. If God said I can bear this, then I can! I seemed to calm down after a while.

I don't know how my son and I got into the car and drove home in that condition. We were both devastated. God was watching out for us - that's for sure! We were both in shock when we got to my mom's house. I walked in and all I could do was shake my head and tell her that the news wasn't good. She helped me through the door and sat me down in the kitchen chair.

A Story of Hate, Love, and Faith

My son was still crying and saying he was going over to his girlfriend's house and to call him if I needed him. He was crying as he left. My mom was trying to make sense of what I told her. She tried to find out from me what the doctor said, but I really couldn't tell her much. I did manage to tell her that I needed surgery to remove my breast. I told her to call the doctor to get more information from him because I didn't remember too much of what he said. I also told her that if the other one was cancerous, he'd take that one, too. I was going through the motions, but wasn't really there emotionally.

I do know I wanted everyone to meet at mom's house that night.

I called my brother in Florida, crying and asking him to come, but he said he wouldn't be able to. He was bawling and couldn't grasp what I was telling him. After we hung up, I pulled myself together and began to figure out what I needed to do to get through this.

My mom was on the phone talking to the doctor while trying to write down everything he was saying - plus, trying to not break down. I told her that if she even started to cry, I'd leave because I needed her to be strong. At that point, I was very scared. I never had surgery in my life, so the thought of it shook me up. She pulled herself together for my sake.

It was strange because a part of me was scared and another part of me was at peace. I knew God was with me and this was His plan. When I thought of that, I calmed down.

What is so ironic is this: My girlfriend's daughter was diagnosed with cancer just two months before me and I was there helping her cope with it when I got the news. By seeing what cancer did to her had an effect on me, but it's not the same when it happens to you.

That night, all of my family was there. They scheduled my surgery for February 22nd, which was two weeks away. I was glad...because I wasn't ready for surgery. The next two weeks, I kept myself busy. A lot of friends came to visit and we prayed...a LOT. I would light candles and we would sit around, see beautiful colors, and pray. I always kept a candle lit at night.

The weekend before surgery, I went to stay with my friend whose daughter had cancer, too. Believe it or not: I never looked at my breast all those months, but I did that day. I had gotten out of the shower and for some reason, I looked in the mirror and really LOOKED at my breast. I got choked up because I could see how sick-looking it was. It was yellow with dents around it - and it was hot to the touch. All I remember saying was, "Poor thing. You really have to come off." I knew it was sick.

Later that night, I took a shower again and all of the sudden, my breast exploded! As soon as the hot water touched my back, I saw this big blob of blood shoot against the wall. Blood was everywhere! I started screaming hysterically for my friend. When she came in, she thought I burned myself with hot water. It was then that she saw all the blood. With a towel wrapped around my head, she rushed me to the hospital at 4:00 in the morning.

When I arrived at the Emergency Room, I was still bleeding. After four hours of waiting, someone finally came in to take care of me. The doctor on call said that I should be alright 'til I have surgery on Monday. They released me and we went home.

When we made it back home, we didn't get much sleep. We were thankful it wasn't serious. I didn't let it get me down. The next night, I went to a house party. Everyone there was praying for me and wishing me the best. I had to be at the hospital early the next day to be prepped for surgery, so I didn't stay too late. It was good seeing friends before I went to surgery.

I slept pretty well that night...considering.

When I arrived at the hospital, all of my family was there - and some of my friends. They stayed with me 'til they wheeled me in to the operating room. To tell the truth: I wasn't scared because I knew God was with me. The operation took two to three hours. In the recovery room, I sat up, looked at my chest, and said, "Not bad" - and then passed out again. When they wheeled me to my room, I was waving my hand saying, "I have one for fun!" They all laughed. As soon as I got to my room, I started walking around. Everybody couldn't believe I just had surgery! I called my brother - and even he couldn't believe it was me!

I owe a lot to God because He really healed me FAST!

At the end of the day, just before I was released, my doctors came in to tell me what my pathology report said. I could tell by the look on their faces that it wasn't good news. One doctor came over to my bed and with his head bowed down, he proceeds to tell me that 19 lymphnodes were full and it had spread to my collarbone. After he was finished, I asked him if I could throw up now. The doctor never gave me any hope. The other doctor raised his hand and said, "Thank God it wasn't anywhere else." THOSE words gave me hope. I grabbed the sheet so tight, my hand turned purple.

I didn't know it then, but the doctor told my family I had only three months to live and to just take me hope and keep me comfortable. Thank GOD I didn't know that - or I would have given up.

After the doctors left, we were getting ready to go home. I couldn't stop crying. I pulled my sister to me and just bawled my eyes out. I heard the lady next to my bed call out to me. She said, "God is with us. I had cancer years ago. Trust in Him." That gave me encouragement, too.

When we got home, everyone broke down - with my permission, of course. My mom has a patio door in the family room, so I went out there by myself to cry. I looked up towards the sky and told God I didn't want to die. I just gave my fears and my heart to God. Still, I couldn't stop crying. After a while, I had peace.

I wanted my son to be there so I could give him the news. My sister called him and he came right over. While I was in the hospital, I talked to a volunteer from the Cancer Society. She had given me a letter to give to my son explaining what families go through when a member has cancer. I told him I had to go see more doctors. I didn't tell him just how bad it was, though. I told him to pray for me - and don't blame God.

After everyone left, I laid down and kept my thoughts on God. I worked on healing myself with thoughts of Him. I would go within and listen to the messages God was speaking to my heart. I believe God sustains us through anything - even illness - no matter how bad…if we just believe.

A Story of Hate, Love, and Faith

My friend's daughter didn't make it. She, however, died believing in God's goodness. She told me that God would heal her, but that in order to save her, they would have to take her leg. She didn't want that. She was only 29 years old. She didn't want to lose her leg, so she passed away - with both of her legs intact.

The next day, they set an appointment for me to see the Oncologists. I didn't know what to expect, so I just went with an open mind. Some of my family came along with me. We were shocked when she said I was a candidate for a transplant and that I would have to take chemo. I felt I was going to do whatever it took! I raised my hand and said, "Let's do this!" My poor family thought that he was going to tell them what the other doctor told them: Even chemo wouldn't save me. Needless to say, they were surprised. Chemo and the transplant were my only hope.

Every week, I had to take chemo right away. I called it 'Kool-Aid'. I told the nurses to call it that, too. My mom said it was Jesus' blood going in my veins. My mom and I each visualized certain things. Then I thought of the Expressway in my mind. It meant that the chemo would skip my organs and go all throughout my body without touching my organs. It worked, too!

The day I lost my hair, I was at my mom's house and she helped me. I cried that day.

Then the nausea started. All I could eat pudding and drink milkshakes. They gave me pills to counteract the chemo. My mom and my older sister would go with me so they could hold my hand. The days I took chemo were rough. For six months, I took chemo.

In July, I was supposed to get my transplant. I looked at the calendar and told myself, "In six weeks, I'll be home." Before the transplant, I had to go to Cleveland a few weeks before so they could harvest my stem cells. My mom, dad, and I went early to Cleveland so they could put a catheter in. It was very painful. When I got back that night, I couldn't sleep because I was in too much pain. God got me through that night. The next time we went to Cleveland, it was just my mom and me. I had to be on this machine for four hours a day for four days. We got a hotel room near the hospital. When I was on the machine, my mom made friends with another lady whose daughter was near me on her own machine. I felt bad for her. Her name was Nancy. Nancy had two things wrong with her: ovarian and breast cancer. We would talk while we were on our machines. She was so sweet. After the four days of treatment were done, we said we would see each other in a couple of weeks (she was also going to have a transplant the same time as me). We then made our way home.

At the end of my catheter, there were three long tubes with a clamp at each end. I had to clean each one separately so I wouldn't get an infection. There were four procedures I had to do for each one. Talk about nerve-wrecking! I was so scared! I shook the whole time. When I saw the needles, I felt like throwing up. I had to practice on an orange. You see, I had to give myself shots in my stomach before my transplant. The nurse said I was doing fine on the orange, but I was not so sure I could do it on my stomach. When she was confident I could manage it, she gave me a week's supply of what I needed. She gave me her number and told me to call if I needed her. I didn't feel as confident in me as she did. I was still scared when I left her office.

A Story of Hate, Love, and Faith

The first day I cleaned my catheter by myself, my sister came over to be with me. My hands shook so bad, I didn't think I could do it. I felt better knowing someone was there in case something went wrong. She watched when I injected the needle in my stomach for the first time. I didn't even think about it: I just stuck it in. I had to do it fast so I wouldn't lose my nerve. I had no other choice because there wasn't anyone else around to do it for me.

One thing I learned throughout this ordeal was that through all of this, you never know what you're capable of doing when the situation is life or death. I had to do a lot of things I didn't think I could do. All I can say is this: I couldn't wait 'til it was all over and things went back to normal.

The two weeks went by fast. I did good giving myself shots. The time came for the transplant. My two sisters and me went to Cleveland to check me in and to stay with me. I was smoking at that time, so when the nurse was done putting the machines on me, when she left, I went into the bathroom to smoke. My nerves were really bad. They said I would get strong chemo - and LOTS of it. I was sick right away. I kept my head covered most of the time. I can't describe how sick I really was. My bowels were inflamed - and I got a yeast infection, too. I was in so much pain, I couldn't talk much. I simply hurt all over.

I was out of it for a while. People would come to Cleveland to see me and all I could do was cover my head.

Every day they came to take me for x-rays and breathing tests, I would get a bloody nose. I was so sick, I just wanted to be left alone. Then at night, they would come to take my blood. When I did sleep, they'd wake me up! My esophagus was burned out, too. I had to drink this liquid 'stuff' so I could heal. One day, I was in the bathroom and couldn't move. The doctor had to remove me. I was in such pain. Funny thing: I never threw up.

Nancy's recovery wasn't going well either. I remember the day of our transplants, I looked over at her and prayed for her. During the night, she died. She had choked on her own blood. There were a lot of people dying around me that night. I was afraid to close my eyes! I felt bad for Nancy's mother. She was there by herself when her daughter passed. The doctor who told me about Nancy dying said that her mother had a sign from God, but didn't say what it was.

What was bad about the process was the chemo. The transplant itself was nothing in comparison. They just put the stem cells back in through the catheter. It is pain-free. See, with chemo, it affects your immune system. You're defenseless, and that's when all kinds of things can happen. I was just one of the 'lucky ones'. I healed very fast - as far as my blood count went. I ended up going home on the date I said I would, but before I could leave, they had to remove my catheter because I was running a fever. I was so scared, they did it in my bed. It was PAINFUL!

My companion came and drove my mom and me home. Would you believe: We had three flat tires on the way! I was so out of it, I didn't care.

A Story of Hate, Love, and Faith

For a whole year, I had fatigue and my esophagus was still burning. I still took medicine for that. I went back to work, but it was too physical. I quit working and went on disability. That happened in 1993. In 2002, I got cancer again - this time, in my right breast. I started losing my hair and had to take chemo again. I was really sick that time, too. I had to have a blood transfusion. The doctor said I was so sick because of all the chemo from before AND now.

I stayed with my sister for five months. I had to have another catheter put in. I snipped it accidentally with scissors and have to have it removed and another put in its place.

I had a lot of peace that time. I knew God would see me through again. I never did have reconstructive surgery, so I buy my boobs every two years. Now, I don't even think of getting cancer again. I just think that if I do get it again, just as it was before, it's God's will.

Darlene S. Watson

Believe Me

I had breast cancer and was given only three months to live (according to man), but you see: That wasn't God's plan.

God says when we're weak, we're strong; that's because God's been with us all along.

I didn't doubt that I was in God's care. He gave me signs that showed me He was there.

The news I heard gave me no hope, but I looked to God to help me cope.

He gave me a peace of mind. I'm glad I called on him in time.

Then the miracle came that gave me a chance: The doctors told me I was a candidate for a transplant!

The chemo they gave me made me so sick. It even made me go out of my head, but I knew without it, I would be dead.

He sent His angels to minister to me. When I felt them and saw them, I was so relieved.

It was my courage - this I knew - but God's love that brought me through.

I couldn't have made it, that's for sure! God is the only One who has the cure.

He strengthened my belief when He pulled me through. I can say he is true blue to me and you!

I'm living proof of what God did for me. He can do the same for you - if you believe.

I thank God with all my heart that He had mercy on me, and in my life I wanted Him to be.

When I found out I was going to die, I sought my God who was stronger than I.

Through it all, He was right there by my side. Without Him, I would have died.

During my illness, I couldn't sit still. I was out doing God's will.

I know what God has done for me. I wouldn't be here if it wasn't for my belief in Him…

A Story of Hate, Love, and Faith

Live by Faith

I think that everyone is afraid to let themselves go. We think too much about what people think rather than what God thinks. God created us so we could live with Him here on the Earth. When we find God, He tells us who we are. We each have our own personality. It's different than all others. God wants to show us the way. As we put our trust in Him, He shows us how to live. He tells us what to do for our sakes. Without God's protection, we're in this world without God's help. The more we walk with God, the more I know His ways. I have to learn to live by faith, but each time, God proves Himself faithful to me. He can be counted on to take care of me. He tests us so we can be our very best. He's our teacher, too. He corrects us when we're wrong or out of balance. With God, it's just like a relationship: The more time you spend with Him, the more you know his ways. It takes time to build trust, but when you know the heart of God, you begin to trust Him completely. When there is a storm, we should always go to God first - instead of people. Half the time, people don't know what they're doing. Only God knows what's going on.

God saves us so that we can know without God in our lives, there is nowhere to go. We can either have His best or we can choose to have our way. I had many problems growing up. I was in constant pain. I had an abusive childhood. When God found me, I was a mess. He convicted me of my sins, and in Him I could begin again. I gave my life over to Him. He has revealed to me the truth about myself and how I stuffed my feelings inside. Once by one, I got free. The truth is what makes us free. God wants me well, and he heals my emotions little by little. He gives me the power to go through each one. The devil likes to see you down. With God's help, we can win! There is a battle going on; that's why we need to run to God.

He teaches me how to treat people and to give my life to the service of others. It is better to give than to receive. God is Love and He wants us to do the same: Love our neighbors like we love ourselves. We should always follow the Golden Rules. God makes me want to do better. I want to be like Him. He is merciful, compassionate, loving, just, and righteous. His mercies are new every day. He corrects me when I've done wrong.

Our feelings are fickle, so we can't rely on them. We live by being instructed from the Word of God. We must be in the Word of God every day to know what His will is for us. I love the Word of God!

God is with me wherever I go. He knows what's up ahead. Our sense of right and wrong are within; God tells us when we sin. If we don't face what we've done, we feel bad. Then there's guilt we can't get rid of, so we ignore the signs. Only God can forgive our sins and make us whole. He died to set us free so we would know without Him, there's nowhere to go. It's not us who searched for Him: He's the One who does the chasing. His gift is free for anyone who believes. He draws us to Him. It's our choice if we receive Him in our hearts.

Sin and the devil are real. We're only safe in God's hands - and that was His plan. When we submit our wills to God, that means He's in charge. I became one of God's children. I put my trust in Him like never before…and He has never let me down. He is faithful to His Word. He's so good to me, I can't explain. I just know I'm not the same. I'm learning to walk by faith each day so I can know my way. I cast my cares on God's shoulders and leave them there so I can live with no stress. He takes my problems so I can rest. We all have a child within us, so we need to bring them out. That is who we really are.

A Story of Hate, Love, and Faith

I've covered up so much of my real self, it took God to help me discover who I really am. I really like myself now and enjoy what I have. I simplified my life down to only what I need. Clutter in your house is clutter in your mind. We can control what thoughts we have. What we think is how we act. Positive words are what builds us up - and negative words tear us down. Did you know that when we speak bad things about someone, we are cursing them? When we speak good words, we bless them! Words are powerful, so we need to be alert about the things we say. When we love our fellow man, we keep God alive. God is Love; that is who He is! He knows each of us by name and (to my surprise) He treats us all the same. Popular belief is that God is cruel and doesn't care. That's a lie people share.

Everyone does what others do and they don't care if it's the right thing to do. I go to God because He knows what to do so that I don't get confused. When God comes to live inside of us, He will keep our minds clear.

Blessings come to those who believe in and obey the Lord. Why do we do the things we hate? We know nothing of who we are. When we're in God, He tells us who we are. God knows me better than I do myself. When you know better, you do better. We are brand new when God comes into our lives. The old has passed away. Even if we have to go through some pain to heal, He gives us the power to overcome. We don't have to stay the way we are. People say, "We can't do this or that". God says, "ALL things are possible". You have to begin to trust yourself; that also means to love yourself. Love is action, not just feelings. You are valuable and worthy. Don't listen to others about yourself: Listen to what God says in His Word about you! Hurting people hurt people and they lash out. Words that were not kind can stay with us for years. They destroy the human heart.

Invest in yourself because all you have is you. Don't be afraid to say what you've done because you can forgive them one by one. You don't have to live in the past - only if you choose not to. Jesus came to set us free. Take a leap of faith and join in, then your new life can begin! Call sin what it is and don't hold back. The truth will set you free! Call on the Lord to help you through; you will find He is true blue. The words we tell ourselves can be just as bad as what we were told. You can be kind to yourself and can stop the negative talk.

We all want to find peace of mind. God is peace, so we must be with the Prince of Peace. Joy is another thing we lack. We try different things that will make us happy - only to discover we're not happy after all. Peace and joy are in the Lord. It is deep within us.

We've been hurt inside so much that we don't know what is there. We stuff away our feelings in order to survive. We numb ourselves from feeling any pain. We're afraid to get close to love again because we were so hurt. We don't even like or love ourselves. We think it's our fault that people abused us. I know I took the blame for many years and felt guilty, too - but when I walled myself in, I walled everyone else out. I was so empty, so lonely inside. I became bitter and on the defense. I would strike out at others with my words and hurt the ones I loved. I was very angry but didn't know it. I had buried it inside so I acted out my feelings...not knowing why. I was in denial for most of my life. The pain was too much to bear at times. I didn't trust anyone, either. I thought I had it all together, then one night I fell apart. I felt someone snatch me up and convict me of all my sins. After that, I felt a peace I never had before. I had the strength to repent. I was forgiven for ALL of my sins.

A Story of Hate, Love, and Faith

I had to clean my slate of all the things I hate. It wasn't easy at first because within, we have to face all our sins. When God brings them out to view, I don't hurt like I used to. I can feel again, and to know that God loves me, I can accept who I am. One by one, I had to face what was destroying me inside. Those were the things I wanted to hide. I was sick inside for a while and didn't know what to do, so I called on God to get me through. I had to face the facts that people you love don't love you. It hurts a lot, but it feels good to break free. I'm healed today because I let God in and showed me what was wrong.

We're all on a journey, so some things are different for each of us. God works on us in our different circumstances. What He works on me might be different for you. One thing is true: He wants to make us brand new. He wants us healthy and whole. It's hard work to want to change, but it is worth it in the end. Only with God's help can change begin. He knows us all too well and can tell us who we really are. God takes us through things day by day and step by step. He doesn't put more on us than we can bear. When we share ourselves, we're learning from each other. We hurt, heal, and help each other.

I found out that working on being whole is a long process. God delivers me little by little. It's hard work to want to change, so you have to be patient with yourself and God. In the Bible, Jesus asked a lot of people if they wanted to be well. I think He's asking us the same question. I was so sick of being sick that I searched for answers that only God could give me. I was in bondage from so many things, I didn't know where to start! Little by little, God took me apart to show me what broke my heart. They were things I never shared with anyone. Only God knew what was making me sick and keeping me bound. I had to clean the slate for all the things I hated. Once I began, there was no turning back.

One by one, I was able to see what was inside of me. It sure made me sick - I'll tell you that! Once I knew the truth, I was set free. I'm still learning the things in my heart that are not right, so to get set free, I put up a fight. When God brings my sins to view, I don't struggle like I used to. It gets better every day, and with God's help, He washes it away. I had so much junk inside, I never thought I would survive. When we stop covering up the way we feel, the we can start on being real. So many masks we wear, just so we can hide who we are. We put up walls to protect ourselves, but then we're walling ourselves in. There are so many phony people around, it makes it hard to relate. There is so much pain inside; that is what drives us wild. Only God can get me through, and in His love, He makes me brand new. When we live for ourselves, we're shallow and empty inside. When we focus on others, that keeps God's love alive. Until I was saved, I lived for myself - and what a mess I was in. Then God came into my life and gave me the courage to repent of all my sins. He forgave me on the SPOT! I have been walking with God for so long and realize I can't live in this world without Him by my side.

A Story of Hate, Love, and Faith

God is the One

We don't understand why He does what He does; whatever the reason, it's because He loves.

He wants us to be the best we can, to rely on Him and not man.

We don't know what plans God has made for us; what gets us through is faith and trust.

God lifts our spirits to new heights. A whole new world is in our sights.

We don't understand the things we're meant to do, but in time He gives us our clue.

We all have a purpose to fulfill; this isn't our plan, but God's will.

God takes care of His own. We do our best 'til He calls us home.

He's the only connecting link that helps sort out the things we think.

There are times God puts us through a test, and that's so we can be our very best.

Trials and tribulations make us strong to teach us to learn what went wrong.

God is helping us correct our mistakes; trials of life is what it takes.

He gives us strength through it all, just so we don't falter and fall.

He can relate to the things we go through; after all, He was once like me and you.

He went through pain and suffered so, just so we would have a place to go.

He saved us all from our sins, and in God, our life begins.

Darlene S. Watson

God's Choice

Whenever we feel sick and feel yuck, that's because of things that keep us stuck. I was stuck for many years. All I did was cry many tears. Then I fell apart. I just couldn't take it anymore. That's when I fell to the floor. I got to my bed and He was there; He gave me peace right away. I told Him all I knew about my sins, and in Him I could live again. I was confused in my mind all the time - not knowing why. He convicted me real hard. I know it gave me the courage to repent. After a while, I felt fine. Even my mind was clear. To this day, I don't know why He chose me, but it's a privilege to serve Him any way I can. He died on the cross for me and you and took all our sins so we could be set free. He healed my broken heart and made me well; I owe Him a lot. This was God's plan for all of us. We don't do a thing: just accept what He did for you and me. He doesn't leave me where I'm at; He's always trying to set things right. God took me from the devil's clutch and freed me from all my sins. I didn't really know that I was a sinner and that I needed a Savior stronger than I. I still sin often; when I ask God to forgive me, He does. The world is full of hate and strife. This isn't what real life is. We need to bring Salvation back with love and peace. God is love and not hate. There is another force of evil that surrounds us on every side. The devil likes us down and out. God wants us strong and free. I take my orders from God. I used to take them from the devil; now I know the difference. God spares my life…the devil destroys it.

A Story of Hate, Love, and Faith

When we walk in darkness and not the light, then we hide who we are. Come to the light of Jesus so you can see what He has done for you and me. We keep secrets, you and I; we don't live in the truth…we live in lies. The truth is what sets us free. Lies keep us bound. Bondage is all the junk we carry that we don't let go of. What helps us is God's love. We have a lot of baggage we carry around, and those things keep us down. God cleans us inside out so we can be brand new. It's worth it in the end because you're set free!

We are all looking for things to make us feel good. We need to know where to look. God is the One who knows what's true and only He can fill our needs.

Everyone does what others do. They don't care if it's the right thing to do. I go to God 'cause He knows what to do so that I don't get confused. When God comes to live inside of us, He gives us the strength to follow Him. He may take us where we've never been before. One good thing: Life is not a bore! When you give up your plans and follow Him, you will be surprised at what He can do.

God is the Creator. He is our Maker. God can make us brand new if we give up what we choose to do. On our own, we can't do much. It is He who makes our lives better. He is our life source. We wouldn't survive without Him. People don't think about that... Each day, there is something new I never knew what it feels so that I could enjoy my day. When we try to control our lives, we're really falling apart. I accept what the day brings, knowing who holds the future. I have let go and let God! I can't believe I've come this far. Hard work is what is takes. I wanted so much to be well. I always searched, just to learn God was with me all along. He's healed my heart like never before. I love Him a lot, that's for sure! I gave up the blame-game, and I'm so glad that I can forgive the ones who hurt me in the past. Once I did that, my healing came very fast. We have to be honest with ourselves in order to be well. It's not easy to start, but it is worth it in the end. We all have bad habits we need to break because our attitudes are at stake. God is the One we look up to when things go wrong. He's the One who makes us strong.

When we put God first, He blesses beyond our wildest dreams. We don't have to worry a lot; He answers our prayers without a doubt. I don't care what people say. I know for sure that God is with me and makes me feel OK. God is the only one who can show us the way; we need to call on Him right away. God cheers me up when I am down. This is what makes me come around! God is for real - I know this for sure. He helped me fight when life was a blur.

Some of us were never loved, so we think that we were at fault. Without love, we don't know that there is a better life for us. First, we have to take apart all the things that broke our hearts. Little by little, I want to know how to break free and know me as God does. Fear is what tears us apart because we're afraid of what's in our hearts.

A Story of Hate, Love, and Faith

Faith and love are what heals our souls. One by one, I want to see what happened to all of me. I had to clean my slate of all the things I hate. Once I began, I felt free. Those were things inside of me. I have a list of what I have done. It isn't the same for everyone. God is the only one I listen to today. He directs me always. He came to save us from ourselves. If we would just begin to trust, then our lives would begin. I was living in sin and didn't take the time to let God in. God showed me a new way to live and helped to cleanse my soul within. I stuffed away a lot when I was young, and that caused me to be stuck. God shows me day by day how I've grown and lets me know that I'm His own. We put ourselves down more than we think; it's what we say to ourselves that stinks. I know because I belittled myself when I was a kid. I blamed myself and took a lot of abuse. I used to think, "What is the use?" I forgot the things I said, but they were still in my head.

I did more damage to myself because I took it out on me. They didn't care that I was hurt. Mean and cruel words they would blurt. It's taken me years to sort through the mess. I can say today I am truly blessed. God will help us be strong to face what went wrong. He's my Father and my Friend, and in Him, we begin again. God has a plan for each one of us and wants us to be our very best. We share with each other what we have learned so they, too, can grow. We're here to help others thrive and that's when we keep love alive. God loves us so much; He really has a loving touch. We are each affected by each other's sorrows, but there's still a great tomorrow.

When we admit we were wrong, we take responsibility for our actions. Then we know we're living right. We're too busy to take the time; that's why we're not fine. God doesn't hurry us along; He takes His time so we can see what we live our lives in a blur. I don't know what I did yesterday 'cause I rushed through. Today, I am calm and know what to do.

Furthermore, through our faith, great things happen to us. Faith is what we believe can happen at any time. The more we step out, the more it becomes real - and the stronger faith becomes. We all have a gift from God that is not the same as everyone else's gift.

God has given me the gift to write. I want to write something that will help others on their journey. We are all in different stages of our lives, but we are on the same path:

Wanting to live a happy, fulfilled life, we must put God at the center of our lives. Only He knows us and the way we were created to be. Left by ourselves, we put up walls and wear masks to hide who we really are. The finding out who we are begins inside. A lot of people don't like what they see, so they are false to you and me. They are afraid that if we really knew them, we would reject or criticize them. Some people don't feel they are worth a thing, and even though God loves them, they don't accept that.

Our worth and value are not what people say they are. God gives us our worth and value. When He created us, it was for His purpose. Since coming to God, I have found my true self. God tells me what I am about, so He helps get it out. Once we know the truth about ourselves, we can work it through. He is here to help us find peace of mind. When I take the time to let Him in, then my peace begins. I was scared at first to begin, but He was with me at that start. I just needed to open up my heart. When we know in our hearts what to do and ignore what is there, we are not being true to ourselves. People tell us what they think is right for us. Do they even know what's right for themselves? We're always with ourselves…we can't escape. We need to pay attention to God's help. Trust God to tell us the truth; after all, He created me and you!

A Story of Hate, Love, and Faith

The Enemy

He's around, lurking in the shadows. We think we know him, but we don't.

He hides himself in so many disguises; that's because he doesn't like us.

One is blame that covers the mess and makes us feel less and less.

Denial keeps us depressed from all the things he wants us to repress.

Shame is pain we won't let go of because we feel we don't deserve to be loved.

He takes us apart bit by bit. Half the time, we don't even know we've been hit.

He laughs at us when we do something wrong. He likes us weak and not strong.

When we're down, feeling low, and not on the go, he's just lying there watching the show.

He's like a prison guard on the alert; if you don't watch for him, he can really hurt.

He acts like a big shot blowing his horn. He promises you roses, then turns them to thorns.

False pride he hides from us because he doesn't want to be seen, so he sabotages our reality.

He dominates our conversation when someone asks us, "Who do you believe in?" - and we hesitate. He has his proof right there that our Heavenly Father's name we won't share.

The world is his classroom and he's the teacher. He hates anyone who stands for the preacher.

Slowly he wins people over to his side, because eventually they believe all his lies.

He walks in darkness because he's not a pretty sight. He stays in the dark and hates the light.

Stealing is another game he spends time doing, and stands back and does all the viewing.

Killing is one of his whims; when it's over, he stands there and grins.

Killing is one of the games he likes to play a lot; he likes to win, so watch out!

To him, life is just casualties of war. When out there on the battlefield, he likes it even more.

So always be on your guard because recognizing him is very hard.

Don't forget there is a war going on and he likes to win. This game he likes is called 'Sin'.

Repent and save yourself from this evil man, and walk together in God's hand.

I know this enemy, you see. He can't fool me because God is the one in whom I believe.

This mysterious man who, on occasion I run into, happens to be the devil, too.

A Story of Hate, Love, and Faith

Teacher

God loves us and wants us to be the very best, and in order for us to keep on our toes, every once in a while, he gives us a test.

He grades us on the work we've done, and gives us scores that aren't the same for everyone.

By our answers we give Him, He knows we did our homework within.

Some people might be average, then some might get Bs; then there are some who flunk all of these.

He coaches them and hears them out, then He lets them figure out what it's all about.

Some students make mistakes over and over again because they're too lazy to do their work. They want someone else to put the time in that it took.

He gives us a new lesson each day. Some do their homework, and some go out to play.

If God was to call on you, would you know the answer? Or would you think it over and say, "I'm not sure". It's your choice if you pass or not; some people skip school an awful lot.

If we skipped over our lessons for that day because we're mad, we say, "Why do we have to bother with that stuff anyways?"

We have to do research on some of our assignments, but we don't have to go too far; a lot of information is inside of us.

Then there are some assignments that take no time at all. Those are the ones we whiz through and learn nothing new.

Some assignments are too hard for us, too; so we take it to the Teacher because He's the only one that knows what to do.

Your Teacher is always there to help you find what you're looking for; just take the time to knock on His door.

Our Teacher is there to help us grow. The lessons he gives us is to see how much we know.

He gives you all the answers all the time, but if you don't pay attention, you forget them over time.

To find the time or place to study is hard these days because we're too preoccupies with our own ways.
A lot of us look up to our Teacher because we know He cares about us because He told us so...

A Story of Hate, Love, and Faith

The Way, The Truth, and Life

We need to bring Salvation back to find the way to get back on track.

Seek the truth and you shall find everlasting life in time.

The Book of Life binds us together as one; thy will be done for everyone.

When we look up to people in power and we do all they say without checking it out, then we put them before God without a doubt.

Duplicating God's image in the likeness of man was man's idea and not God's plan.

It is plain to see we don't honor God when we use His name in vain; as a matter-of-fact, He will treat us the same.

We don't know what God has to say when we do our chores on the Sabbath Day.

When our father and mother help us out of love and we put up resistance, then we need to keep our distance.

We want out of our cage when we kill someone out of our pent up rage.

When there is an act of love between two people unseen, this act is nothing but adultery.

Taking something that doesn't belong to us is stealing; taking it without permission is very appealing.

If we know the truth about someone and we don't reveal it to someone else, then we bear false witness.

If we desire the things that don't belong to you and me, it is called envy.

Friends

Friends are the ones we keep close to our hearts and are there for us when we fall apart.

A friend is honest with you, even if it hurts you, too.

Friends will listen and do all they can; most of all, they understand.

They see the good, bad, and ugly - and still accept me for me.

With friends, we can be who we are, even though that's sometimes hard.

Friends help out with our tasks and don't hesitate when we ask.

We are connected by a link; that's because we love each other...I think.

We can't go very far in life without a friend because when we're down, they pick us up again.

Then sometimes without reason or rhyme, they seem to know you need them and get there in the nick of time.

Friends never give up on us even if we've had a bad day. They know in time, it will pass away.

Our friends are there to encourage us to be all that we can be - out of love and not jealousy.

Our friends make us feel we belong because they don't judge us when we do something wrong.

They build us up so we can grow and give advice on what they know.

They speak the truth and never lie. This is a friend to you and I.

We tell secrets to our friends because we know they will never tell a single soul.

Sometimes we just need a shoulder to cry on, just to be there and not to respond.

They help us through the good times and the bad - that's for sure! Without friends, they would be hard to endure.

Unconditional love is what friendships are made of.

Friends are hidden treasures that are hard to find these days. If you have friends, keep them in your heart always.

A Story of Hate, Love, and Faith

Family

Family patterns are hard to break. Hard work is what it takes.

Our past hinders us more than we think; we have to change in order to break the link.

We can't choose our families, but we can choose to be what we want to be.

When some don't conform to patterns carried down from generations, it can rock the family foundation.

When your beliefs are different from theirs, they'll say it's because we don't care.

Just because you don't see things the way they do, they think something's wrong with you.

You try to do what you can, but after a while, you have to make a stand - because after a while, you're back to where you started, then you feel like a martyr.

Sometimes you have to estrange yourself from a situation that's not good for you, even if it's family you're close to.

Working on the inside is where you begin; gradually, over time, you'll find peace within.

It is not easy to be your own person because some people sabotage your growth - that's for certain!

It is hard to change when they stay the same. When something goes wrong, you still take the blame.

You have to want to change in order to begin; it's not on the outside, but within.

It is hard at first because we don't know what is there. Their own feelings we never share.

They are a part of who we are; if neglected, they leave you scarred.

Peace doesn't come right away. You have to work at it day by day.

Stay focused on what is important for you to grow so you can help others who don't know.

I can tell you it's hard to do, but it sure feels good once you break through!

A Story of Hate, Love, and Faith

Undercover

When I was three, my mom brought this man down to the farm and introduced him to us.

He was so nice to me; I wanted him to be my daddy.

He came down a lot and stayed there, too; my love for him grew.

My Uncle Ben was a carpenter, too. The man owned a bar and gave him work to do.

He and my Uncle Ben were friends even then.

When I saw all four of them in their disguises, my fear was sinking in. My mistrust of him started to begin.

The voice I heard scared me the most. He was one of them who gave a toast.

"Little girl, little girl", went the sound. I knew that voice because he had started to come around.

He wore a ring that I saw before; he scared me to the core.

He thought he was safe undercover, but I knew he was going with my mother.

There were four of them from the start; that man was one of them who broke my heart.

He treated my mom mean, too; he did a lot of evil things, too.

He acted like a big shot when he'd come down and bossed us around.

Four men took me to a shack in a sack.

They laid me on a table. I tried to get up, but I wasn't able.

The man always wore starched shirts. What he did to me was the worst.

He took my legs and spread them apart, then did things to me that killed my heart.

They all took turns with me that day. It was the month of May.

They put a knife close to my belly. I was so scared, I shook like jelly.

When he came on top of me, I screamed hysterically when he entered me.

They sat me up when they were through and mixed me up on what I knew.

When I came to, grandma was there. All I could do was stare.

I bawled my brains out and told her what that man was all about.

She told me to shut my mouth if I know what's good for me; she didn't care that they raped me.

Becky was there, too. She passed out, is all I knew.

They dropped us three in a place and left us there without a trace.

Mom, by then, was big and slim. She had a baby within.

The man was seeing my Aunt Bea, too; they were together in my view.

They got mad because I saw them like that; that went behind my mom's back.

He called me a "big mouth", too, just because I saw the things he'd like to do.

He always flashed his money when he'd come down. He did it a lot when we were around.

A lot of times, mom was his partner in this. "Why can't she get rid of him?" I would wish.

Undercover II

He can be very nice. Yes, he can! But I lived with this evil man.

He always wanted to get in my pants; he would try when he'd have a chance.

I started hating him then; the things he did to me with my Uncle Ben.

When I'd run to my mom because I was afraid of him, she'd cover it up all over again.

His secret was safe with me because I couldn't hurt him like he hurt me.

He belonged to a club called The Knights of Columbus, too. I met a lot of his family through them.

They were gamblers, too, and made bets on the horses - like gamblers do!

When my mom married him, I knew our life was going to be very grim…

Darlene S. Watson

Impostor

When my dad messed with me, it was never the same; she made it worse for me because I took the blame.

All those years were really bad, all because of a man I called 'dad'.

He told me, too, that I wasn't his blood - so no big deal. When he said that, I saw him for real.

He told me that he always fantasized about me and that I better not tell Sally and Susan.

He played the role of a good dad; behind closed doors, he was bad.

He put a roof over our heads; all he wanted was to get me in bed.

He made threats to me when I was full-grown, and told me I better watch it when I was alone.

He was always sneaky and spying on me. Why can't he just let me be?

He would tell me the things my mom would say about me. He didn't care if it hurt me deeply.

He told me, too, how she put him through Hell because of me. I took the blame - like always.

All good memories I have of him are few and far in between; all I wanted was to get out of that scene.

He was an impostor who pretended to be my dad. He ruined the relationship we once had.

He crossed the line that fathers shouldn't do; all he cared about is what he wanted from you.

He used love to gain my trust. I found out later, it was only lust.

My mom knew what he had done; when she turned on me, he knew he had won.

He used me in the worst way; my feelings for him have all gone away.

With God's help, I can be free from the past...

To heal from the pain at last.

A Story of Hate, Love, and Faith

A J

A J I called her then. When she came around, I never knew when.

She never came down to visit with me. All she wanted was to party.

She didn't care that I loved her so; she was too busy to want to know.

A J made me sick. All the mean things she'd say did stick.

She ignored me all the time when she came down. She had even knocked me to the ground.

All the lies you're telling me - I don't believe you. You're a liar and crazy, too!

I wouldn't let up on the things I saw, not even the things about grandma.

She was hateful even then; she wouldn't even protect me from Uncle Ben.

She knew what they were doing all along; she hated me for being headstrong.

She'd rant and rave like Uncle Ben; she couldn't stand my mouth even then.

I'd run to her because she was my mother, but all she did was defend her brother.

The things I told her made her mad. She yelled at me and made me sad.

She turned on me like they all did, and she was my mother - and I, her kid.

I was afraid of her when she acted like them, so I'd run and hide - and just cried and cried.

The look she gave me scared me a lot. A nervous stomach is what I got.

She didn't have to say a word - her look said it all: "Leave me alone! I'm having a ball!"

She would always give me that look; seeing her face, I shook and shook.

The hurt I felt was really deep. She took sides with the creep.
There was Hell to pay when I'd tell her the scoop; she is also one who hurt Whoop the Snoop.
A J wasn't around very much. She never had a loving touch.
She'd grab my arm real rough and get mad when I acted tough.
She didn't want to hear what I had to say; she never spent the whole day.
She didn't care what they did to me; all she wanted was for me to let things be.
She'd tell me I was making up stories that weren't true. She was mad because I knew.
She'd look real mean most of the time. She didn't care if I was fine.
I thought she'd help me once she knew, but I found out she was true blue - that scared me, too.
She didn't like it when I told her about family. Instead of turning on them, she turned on me.
They liked it when she took their side, and when she did, I cried and cried.
I had no one to turn to. After that, I wouldn't tell the things they'd do.
A J was really mean. She never took us out of that scene...

A Story of Hate, Love, and Faith

God Zapped Me Away

Tied my hands to the bed. Put the wire on my head.

A stick in my mouth so I couldn't scream. Get me out of this dream.

The current hit so hard, I saw stars.

They scrambled my brain so I couldn't remember a thing…but I saw his ring.

He was in a white coat. He said I was his scapegoat.

Uncle Ted was a mad scientist; he talked with a lisp.

Men in white coats took me away one December day.

I was put in isolation until I was stable; I was on a cold table.

His eyes were red, his lips were curled, sick words he hurled.

He was possessed by the devil - I could see that; I saw the beast - and that's a fact!

Jeff's shack is where he zapped me.

He took a drill to my teeth and kept it up until I would bleed.

Ted was a madman and used me for his plan.

My body twitched when he turned the machine on. I fell off the table and hit the ground. I laid there without making a sound.

He shamed me there, too; I called him "Daddy Do".

The four of them were there that day when God zapped me away!

He went and got a knife then circled it around my middle - then he talks to me in a riddle.

He's going to stab me there! I blocked out his mean stare.

Sam-Sam, you dirty old man and Clarence was my mom's cousin, you see.

He took his snake out of me and wiped it on my leg. "Get it out!" I beg.

A minister dressed in black held me down in that shack.

A woman was there saying, "Do it! Do it!" Aunt Julie tortured me.

She scraped my insides until I passed out; when I came to, there was only two.

I opened my eyes and told them, "God will punish you for this!"

I couldn't move - my guts hurt so bad. One of the men was dad.

I was bleeding and couldn't move; I was so dazed, I didn't know who was who!

Debbie's eyes were rolling in her head; she laid there almost dead.

We both crawled because we couldn't walk; we were crying so hard, we couldn't talk.

When we got to grandma's, all we did was stare into space. She cleaned me up and left not a trace.

Jeff's shack was their meeting place, so they could hide all the evil things they used inside.

Different Folks

They would create Adam and Eve - the whole scene.

They played the part of Moses with the Ten Commandments, too; we had to obey the Golden Rule.

They were Ku Klux Klan; they killed a black man, too.

They played human games with this man. We had to find his missing hand.

They'd line their beer bottles up like bowling pins, and with his head we knocked them dead.

I tried and tried to swallow his eye.

They had war games, too. Our trainer was someone we knew.

They'd tie a rope from tree to tree; monkey see, monkey do - Debbie, Pat, and me.

We had to hang on until we got to the end. We were exhausted by then.

Then we had to find body parts; one of them was a human heart.

We'd each get a clue on what to do; we couldn't come back 'til we were through.

They'd take us in the woods late at night and leave us there. It was scary, but they didn't care.

They'd take us to the store and tell us a clue; if we could find it, they left you.

They played school a lot, too, and mix you up on what you knew.

They take the letters and change the words; this is the way we learned.

Their family all lived close together on their farms; that's why they did things without harm.

They were all related in some way, and at their house we went to pray.

They would tell us to look in their 'bible' and repeat after them. If we didn't, we'd have to do it all over again.

They put us through this a lot; if we couldn't do it, punishment is what we got.

They used the zodiac signs to predict the future on what they should do.

They were good with their craft; they also dealt in witchcraft.

They would do magic before our eyes and put us under a spell with their surprise.

Psalm 30

I will extol thee, O Lord; for thou hast lifted me up, and hast not made my foes to rejoice over me.

O Lord my God, I cried unto thee, and thou hast healed me.

O Lord, thou hast brought up my soul from the grave: thou hast kept me alive, that I should not go down to the pit.

Sing unto the Lord, O ye saints of his, and give thanks at the remembrance of his holiness.

For his anger endureth but a moment; in his favor is life: weeping may endure for a night, but joy cometh in the morning.

And in my prosperity I said, I shall never be moved.

Lord, by the favor thou hast made my mountain to stand strong: thou didst hide thy face, and I was troubled.

I cried to thee, O Lord; and unto the Lord I made supplication.

What profit is there in my blood, when I go down to the pit? Shall the dust praise thee? Shall it declare thy truth?

Hear, O Lord, and have mercy upon me: Lord, be thou my helper.

Thou hast turned for me my mourning into dancing: thou hast put off my sackcloth, and girded me with gladness;

To the end that my glory may sing praise to thee, and not be silent.

O Lord my God, I will give thanks unto thee forever.

Psalm 31

In thee, O Lord, do I put my trust; let me never be ashamed: deliver me in thy righteousness.

Bow down thine ear to me; deliver me speedily: be thou my strong rock, for an house of defense to save me.

For thou art my rock and my fortress; therefore, for thy namesake lead me, and guide me.

Pull me out of the net that they have laid privily for me; for thou art my strength.

Into thine hand I commit my spirit: thou hast redeemed me, O Lord God of truth.

I have hated them that regard lying vanities: but I trust in the Lord.

I will be glad and rejoice in thy mercy: for thou hast considered my trouble; thou hast known my soul in adversities.

And hast not shut me up into the hand of the enemy; thou hast set my feet in a large room.

Have mercy upon me, O Lord, for I am in trouble: mine eye is consumed with grief, yea, my soul and my belly.

For my life is spent with grief, and my years with sighing: my strength faileth because of mine iniquity, and my bones are consumed.

I was a reproach among all my neighbors, and a fear to mine acquaintance: they that did see me without fled from me.

I am forgotten as a dead man out of mind: I am like a broken vessel.

For I have heard the slander of many: fear was on every side: while they took counsel together against me, they devised to take away my life.

But I trusted in thee, O Lord: I said, Thou art my God.

My times are in thy hand: deliver me from the hand of mine enemies, and from them that persecute me.

Make thy face to shine upon thy servant: save me for thy mercies sake.

Let me not be ashamed, O Lord; for I have called upon thee: let the wicked be ashamed, and let them be silent in the grave.

Let the lying lips be put to silence; which speak grievous things proudly and contemptuously against the righteous.

Blessed be the Lord: for he hath shewed me his marvelous kindness in a strong city.

O love the Lord, all ye his saints: for the Lord persevereth the faithful, and plentifully rewardeth the proud doer.

Be of good courage, and he shall strengthen your heart, all ye that hope in the Lord.

The Bible

'Lilies of the Valley' they'd call their spread. Out of the book this was read.

A yoke is a burden we carry for God; my back hurt with their rod.

A token of identity that verifies you and me - Solomon's seal is real.

Noah's Ark when he took spades; they were nigger slaves.

Moses was a deadly man who God couldn't stand.

Adam and Eve were like me and you; they listened to the devil, too.

The Ten Commandments are for our use, so when we punish you without no excuse.

I am your God: Repeat after me. I am the head of my sheep, now repeat after me.

666 is the Antichrist; he's the opposite of Jesus Christ.

Special anniversary is a jubilee on the night the devil is free.

Seal something with a pledge; the devil's mark is on their foreheads.

Reap what you sow; forget the things you know.

See no evil, hear no evil, speak no evil; what you see isn't real.

You are the seed of our ancestry. This book passes through our families.

This book tells our history, and that's why it's a mystery.

There's watchmen who watch what you do so you don't break our rules.

We are the authority, not God - so you are to give us the glory.

I am the master of all things; you are one of our offsprings.

One generation goes and another comes. We worship the moon and the sun.

The wise man walks in darkness, and the foolish man talks about holiness.

The seven deadly sins will do you in.

A Story of Hate, Love, and Faith

There is a reason for every season. Spring is when people die when they tell lies.

Summer is when we worship the sun and moon, and harvest, too.

Fall is for people who waste no time in covering up their crime.

The sun is our witness on what you do; the night is to punish you.

This is our kingdom and you must follow our rules; that's why they were so cruel.

You kids will worship me on the seventh day of the month and do as I say on this day.

Sin offerings are two kids: a billy goat and one scapegoat. I was the scapegoat; don't you know?

Pat was the billy goat and I was the scapegoat.

Whatever sin was done that day, I paid a high price that day.

We were called goats for a burnt offering. I couldn't stop coughing.

Debbie and I were yoked together by belts of leather; they had it around our necks just to oppress.

The Old Testament is what they lived by. It gave me a lot of answers to why...

Darlene S. Watson

The Preacher

The head of the sheep was the preacher, Uncle Ben.

He preached the gospel, but put his words in instead.

We worshipped the devil; they would chant and chant.

They preached how God was mean and cruel; I'd think to myself, "What a FOOL!"

When he'd say terrible things about my God, I would be mad. When he shut up, I was glad.

Their church was for all of their family members. I hated that church - I remember.

He didn't preach anything of God while we were there; in a daze I would sit and stare.

I'll block him out whenever I could. After a while, I got good.

They'd have ceremonies to honor the devil. The things they did were so evil!

He'd mix us up on good and bad, and when he talked about God, I was sad.

He liked to "play God", too; so after a while, we didn't know who was who.

He was our master and we were his slaves. If we didn't do what he said, he'd put us in a grave.

He preached with rage in his voice; we didn't want to be there, but we had no choice.

Their church was small, but they didn't care. The family were the only ones there.

He'd put us in caskets, too, and shut the lid. He enjoyed everything he did.

He had his own bible in his hand; half of it, I couldn't stand!

He wrote words that were dirty, too; it made me sick, I tell you!

We would sit in the pews crying a lot because we knew punishment is what we got.

We couldn't escape if we tried. If we did, we would be hung up high.

There was the three of us against all of them; God helped us survive time and again.

He would preach a subject to give them a sample, then torture us for an example.

They all laughed and sneered at our pain; just hearing them told me they were insane.

They'd give us drugs to keep us under control and so we would do what we were told.

They tied us up to make their point, then they'd laugh from their joint.

The proper ones were the worst to me because they pretended to believe and I knew the difference, you see.

They'd pinch us if we couldn't sit still and shook us if we slumped from their pill.

When we were alone - Debbie, Pat, and I - all we could do was cry and cry.

Then we'd laugh to make ourselves feel good. We'd do that a lot whenever we could.

Prisoner of War

He took me to the cellar and shackled me there. It was dark with no light anywhere.

He said, "You're in solitary confinement because you can't keep your big mouth shut." Fear gripped my gut.

The jail was the cellar underneath the house; I was the only mouse.

The jail was damp and musty, too. There was nothing I could do!

Bread and water is all I got on my plate. It was shoved under the gate.

It was a makeshift jail - the gate was to make it seem real.

The cellar was a spooky place; I shook so bad, my heart would race.

He laid the law down in his booming voice - I had no choice.

I told on him again, so he locked me in.

This place was so dark, I couldn't find my God. I thought I was in Hell.

They liked putting me in Hell because I would tell.

This thing they put me in was hung high. I couldn't touch the floor if I tried.

Loops for my arms and one for my head; this is for getting out of bed!

I looked around, hoping I was found.

Will grandma find me? I prayed desperately.

Mad Hatter made me pay for a crime - big time!

I was in there for a week. When he let me down, I was real weak.

I was a pretty sight; I cried from my fright.

My hair was dirty and I smelled, too; that's from going number two.

My pants were soaked from my pee…they degraded me!

I cried all night from my fright.

Grandma covered up for him again and told me that I had sinned!

I couldn't move for days because my back felt broke; that was from their makeshift yoke.

I cried from the spasm in my back from being hung up that week - all because I took a peek.

I went to my hill to be with my God. He took care of me tenderly.

I'd go up there a lot and cry from pain and tell God they were the blame.

I wouldn't cry in front of them because I wouldn't give in.

When they were done with me, I'd go tell Debbie and Pat.

Then we'd huddle and cry - and ask each other: "Why? Why? Why?"

Darlene S. Watson

Insane

Taunting voices all around. I blocked them out because I didn't like the sound.

"Little girl, little girl: Who is going to save you now?" I knew God would somehow.

I messed my pants when they hung me up high. I cried, "Why? Why?"

They took my clothes off so they could see how much more they were going to do to me.

They're poking and pinching me. When I scream, they're laughing.

I was hanging on and crying, too; I was so scared of what they were going to do.

They wiped crap all over me, just so they could humiliate me.

Then they made me eat it while they peed on me and made me drink it - and told me it was my cleansing.

They told me it was parts of God and I better - or else I'd be hit with a belt.

I was still hung up high above the ground. I was in such pain, I couldn't keep my head from falling down.

I felt excruciating pain in my back and arms, begging them to let me down.

I kept saying in my mind, "Hang on. It will be over soon." I remember it was in the afternoon.

My hearing's dull and my body is numb, but my mind was alert. "They were so evil", I would blurt.

This is torture - time for pain - because I spoke Jesus' name.

They put a blindfold on my face and circled me. They wouldn't let me be.

They poked me in my rectum while they were laughing at me. They thought it was funny because I was bleeding.

I'm on my hands and knees when they let me down - and laughed at me when I crawled around.

I'm crawling and bawling, begging them to let me go. "We're not done with you yet; don't you know?"

They laid me down and spread my arms. My feet they tied so I could be crucified.

They hated Jesus and wanted me to feel the pain He did because they hated me, too, when I was a kid.

They'd brainwash me to mix up on who they believe, but I still knew: they worshipped the devil through and through.

After a while, I didn't know my name. All I felt was the pain.

I was so scared, I shook with fright. They would do this night after night.

If I saw something I wasn't supposed to see, they would torture me.

I suffered a lot because I loved God and He loved me. They hated me because I believed…

Darlene S. Watson

When I Needed God

When I was young and in my prime, I knew God was there, but I didn't take the time.

He was my Father and my Friend, but I didn't know much about Him then.

I knew God was there, but I didn't see how much He had already done for me.

All the time, I was living a lie - never knowing the reasons why.

I thought I was good in my own way, and that belief caused me to stray.

You see, it's not our way that brings us peace: It's surrendering our will to do as we please.

I was so tormented and hurting inside, I knew I needed someone stronger than I.

When I couldn't take the pain any more, I called on God like I did before.

Only this time, there was a change in me; I pleaded to him to set me free.

I saw the Holy Spirit come into me; I knew then He heard my plea.

I didn't know at first what it meant. I do know it gave me the courage to repent.

I told God all the things I knew I had done, and by doing that, my peace begun.

I asked God to forgive me and into my life I wanted God to be.

I wanted peace in my life that only God could give and a chance to start all over again.

I thought I was safe behind my wall, but the only one who was hurting was me most of all.

When I Needed God II

When I opened my heart and mind to Him, I was cleansed of all my sins.

I felt my burdens lifting from me; telling the truth does set you free!

All the time, He was showing me how much He cares. I was going about my life unaware.

Knowing God and Living God is what I didn't understand, that living in God is His plan and not man.

I gave myself to God then and there and put my trust in His care.

I needed Him to set me straight on all the things inside of me I hate.

Once He started, there was no turning back. He was showing me the things I lacked.

At first, I put up a fight because it's not easy to set things right.

I don't like the things I see, but I know in time, I'll feel the change in me.

When God brings my sins for me to view, I don't fight it as much as I used to.

It gets easier as I go along. With God's help, I see things I do wrong.

It's a process I must take, so I can correct my mistakes.

A changes begins once we know that without God, there's nowhere to go.

I've come to know God more each day, and in my heart, I know He's showing me the way.

"But seek ye first
the Kingdom of God,
and His justice,
and all these things
shall be added unto you."
Matthew 6:33

"Trust in the Lord
with all thy heart;
and lean not unto thine
own understanding."

Proverbs 3:5

Darlene S. Watson

My Father

I was in too much pain to really know that all God wanted to do for me was show me the way to go.

I lived in pain most of every day; all God wanted to do was make it go away.

He doesn't push Himself on us because He gives us a choice: listen to people or to His voice.

You see, it's a choice on our part if we want to make a clean start.

He knows what we do; he just wants you to know it, too.

With God, we can't go very far if we still want to be who we are.

We fool ourselves if we think we can. God said, "Follow Me; not man."

If we deny Him, then all we're doing is living in sin.

When He says, "The truth will set you free", it means, "Surrender yourself and follow Me."

He has so much to give to us; all He asks is for us to trust.

He wants us to repent of our sins, so in Him we can live again.

It's telling God that we made mistakes and want to be forgiven for our sake.

We don't have to worry on the things we used to do. If we ask God into our lives, He can make us brand new.

God is the only one who knows the way; we need to call on Him right away.

I have a list of the things I know He's done for me, and this is what makes me believe.

He answers all my prayers in due time; if He doesn't answer all of them, it's not a crime.

I might think I need this or that, but He knows best - a lot of times, it's for a test.

He wants us to have patience to endure in order for us to mature.

He's kind, compassionate, and sincere. Without a doubt, He's always near.

He's like a father who loves his own; He guides and protects us 'til he calls us home.

A Story of Hate, Love, and Faith

I've come a long way from that scared little girl; God opened my eyes to a whole new world.

He wants me to know what's real and to stop covering up the way I feel.

He has done so much for me, that without Him I don't know where I'd be.

He teaches me more about Him every day. We have a personal relationship in our own way.

Compassion

When we ask out of curiosity and someone takes time to explain, they show us courtesy.

When we have a bad day and walk in the door, a kind word or a hug lifts us up even more.

When we are too tired after working all day, it feels so good when they ask us if we're OK.

When someone is lonely, we make the time; after a while, they feel fine.

When someone needs a helping hand, we try our best to do what we can.

When we help someone who feels unsure, we love to give them an encouraging word.

When we're unsure and have to think twice, we go to someone we trust for advice.

When we know someone who is down on their luck, we help them out with a few bucks so they won't feel stuck.

When you give a gift from your heart, your kindness will never part.

When you show kindness to young and old, you have a heart of gold.

When you give to the poor who are in need, you set an example of God, indeed!

Owning up to what we do shows people that we have integrity, too.

When we have something nice to say, we lift their spirits in a new way.

When we compliment others on what we see, it helps build up their self-esteem.

When we say 'no' to our kids, it's tough; sticking to it is tough love.

When we give our parents due respect, loving responses are what we'll get.

When we treat all people with respect and love, then we're setting a good example of God's love...

Darlene S. Watson

Looking to God

There is a little child in all of us, all wanting love and trust.

God is our strength through all our pain; knowing this, peace inside I gain.

To gain control in our lives each day, we have to look to God to show us the way.

He can help us focus on what we need to do, so all thoughts of God can come through.

He is our Father from above, and all he wants to do is help us through with His love.

Turn from your sins, the look up and ask Him in.

He loves us so much, he helps us all the way; that is how we made it through the day.

God helps us, no matter what we face. In our hearts, we give Him grace.

We should be still and listen within, then ask Him to forgive our sins.

Don't be afraid to discern what is right. We are called to be salt and light.

When we feel good inside, He is there. He lets us know He truly cares.

We owe Him so much; all He asks is for us to trust.

We should give credit to Him in everything we do; it's because of Him that we're forgiven and made new.

Look in your heart and try to find what will give you peace of mind - then focus on God and not yourself…

A Story of Hate, Love, and Faith

Dad

Dad, I wanted you to know how good you are, so this is from your daughter Dar.

I could never put into words all your generosity or all the things you've done for me.

So I thought I'd take the time and tell you a few.

You always helped people who needed you, never questioning if it was what you should do.

You are so easy to talk to, and we'd have a lot of talks - me and you.

Any time I needed your help, you were right there; even early in the morning when I needed a ride, you didn't care.

The times I'd stop after work and you'd say, "Stay and eat", and I'd say, "No, I gotta go", that was nice, too - I want you to know.

If someone needed you and you were tired, too, you'd still be there - no matter what we asked you to do.

You always taught me that to give is better than to receive. I like that about you, as a matter-of-fact.

At times, you'd give me advice on what I should do. If I didn't agree, I'd tell you, too.

You never got made because I disagreed with what you thought; having an opinion is what you taught.

Through all your struggles and pain, I hardly ever heard you complain.

Your faith and trust sets a good example for the rest of us.

The times you were so bad, I'd say, "I don't think I could endure"; you showed me your strength, that's for sure!

Then when I got sick and you prayed for me, too - with your faith, you helped me pull through.

With all the things that have happened to you, I think your positive attitude and your faith pulled you through.

You held on for our sake, and we could see how much love you have for your family.

Darlene S. Watson

Dad, I just wanted you to know that I love you and that you're in my heart and prayers, too.

Love from your Daughter, Dar

A Story of Hate, Love, and Faith

Diane

I wanted to take the time to say that you're so nice in your own way.

I love you a lot, I want you to know, and this letter is to tell you so.

We've been through so many things with each other, that sometimes I feel I'm your mother.

We have a bond no one else shares 'cause we went through the hard times when no one else was there.

I know some things are hard for you to take when things happen to me, but I know in your heart that you love me deeply.

When I was getting my chemo, I held your hand so tight; it helped me relax 'cause I sure was uptight.

You help up for the love of me; if you were scared, you didn't let me see.

There were times I had nobody and you'd appear, if only just to lend me your ear.

After my catheter was put in and I was scared, I settled down 'cause you were there.

Then when I was so sick, I couldn't walk nor talk when I came home, that's another time you wouldn't leave me alone.

The time I stayed at mom's house 'cause I was so weak, you came over and cooked dinner for us to eat.

The day of John's party when I was really sick, without asking, you came over really quick.

When you stayed with me overnight 'cause I was in such fright, you made me feel everything was alright.

Then when I was out of sorts one day and you didn't know what to say, you came over and brought me that sleigh.

Then the tree you made for me, just so I wouldn't have to spend money.

Through the good and bad that we shared, I know in your heart you truly cared.

So always remember that I love you and will always be there for you, too.

Love from your Sister Dar

A Story of Hate, Love, and Faith

Dan

Dan, this is a message just for you, letting you know the good things - so many memories of me and you. I just wanted to tell you a few.

The times we laughed and cried a lot, those were the times we got chewed out.

We stuck together like glue whenever we had things to do.

You were always my best friend because you knew me so well; all the things I told you, you never tell.

We had a lot of friends in those days and wanted to hang out with them always.

You and I are close - I think of us as one. When I think of you, I get lonesome.

The time it snowed so much and we stood outside to see, the only two people around were you and me.

Then on New Year's Eve, we'd bang our pots and pans; we'd bang 'em as loud as we could stand.

Wherever we would trod, we were like two peas in a pod.

Then last year when I was sick and you couldn't come home, I still felt you with me - even on the phone.

You cried so hard, you couldn't stop - and neither could I. You helped me there because I needed a good cry.

I knew the news hit you pretty hard, but you were with me through your cards.

When I came to see you and you told everybody you were there to take care of me, you took charge just so I wouldn't have to worry.

When we'd stay up and talk through the night and you got a message that I was going to be alright.

The day we were packing and we cried and cried, we didn't get much done - even though we tried!

Then the day I thought I needed a transfusion, you settled me down 'cause I was in confusion.

Then the songs you sent me made me cry even more; they made me cry like I did before.

Then the night we danced - you and I - I didn't want to have to say good-bye.

So Dan, I wanted you to know from me that these things were all out of love for me.

Always remember that I love you so, and I just wanted to tell you so.

Love from your Sister Dar

A Story of Hate, Love, and Faith

Russ

This is from you sister Dar, just to tell you how good you are.

Anytime I needed your help, you'd be right there - no matter what it was, you didn't care.

You're smart: Did you know that? Not much fools you, as a matter-of-fact!

You always gave me compliments and told me I looked good; even if you had a bad day, you would.

The gifts you bought me at Christmas were so fine; they were so nice all the time.

When I would come through the door, you had a hug and a kiss for me in store.

The times you'd call and say, "Talk to me" - I knew those times, you were lonely.

You are so respectful to other people and always set a good example.

You do a lot for your friends - sometimes too much - but that's because you care about them a big bunch.

You help people with your kindness more than you think; a lot of times, it's because they're weak.

You know so many people because you care about everybody, and you'd always say they were your buddies.

When I had trouble with my car, you'd do what you could; and if you couldn't, you'd find someone who could.

The day you came to cut my grass and you couldn't do it, you told Dave to go ahead; and when I gave you the money, you gave it to Dave, instead.

You're so good with all you do; that's why people think so much of you.

You always greet people with a smile and a handshake. You always took time for their sake.

When I got sick and you were afraid, you kept me alive, too, when you prayed.

You give yourself completely to others who are in need; you are a true human being, indeed.

You have a heart as big as gold, and I just wanted to tell you so.

You're very close to my heart, I want you to know - and that I really love you so.

This person I love - because of the things he does - happens to be my brother Russ.

Always remember that I love you and will always be there for you, too.

Love from your Sister Dar

A Story of Hate, Love, and Faith

Lori

This is from your sister Dar, just to tell you how sweet you are. Whether you know it or not, these things meant a lot to me and will always be in my memory.

The times when I was upset and would talk to you, you took time to listen - even though you had things to do.

They probably didn't make sense to you, but you sat there and listened 'til I was through.

You never gave advice on what I had to say; all I wanted was for you to listen anyways.

You always talked good about everyone. As a matter-of-fact, I always admired you for that.

Remember the time I thought John was missing and was upset? You stayed up all night with me without any rest.

Then the time I wasn't good 'mentally'; you sent a card letting me know you were thinking of me.

Then my first day back to work, you took the time and came to see if I was fine.

Then when I got sick last year, you gave me money to take to Florida with me and said, "Have a good time and don't worry."

Then that night in the hospital when I wasn't so good, you held my hand and comforted me the best you could.

That same night, you stayed with me. You didn't know it, but I was scared; you helped me a lot by being there.

I love you, Lori, and I want you to know: In your own way, you've helped me grow.

I know you'd be there if I asked you to; that's how much I know about you.

You're in my thoughts, even when I don't see you. I want you to know I pray for your family, too.

Darlene S. Watson

This person who is very dear to me happens to be my sister Lori. Always remember that I love you and will always be there for you, too.

Love from your Sister Dar

A Story of Hate, Love, and Faith

Jo

I can remember so many nice things about you. I thought I'd take the time to tell you.

I never asked you for help, but somehow you must have read my mind. Without knowing it, you got to me in the nick of time.

The time I took my house back and I was down, you came over and brought me around.

I didn't have any food either that day; it touched my heart that you went out of your way.

Then there was the time I was staying at Diane's and was so depressed; you brought me a book and lifted me up again.

You always did something for me on my birthday. I still remember them today.

I always lived my life through you, would you believe? Because a lot of things I was afraid of for me.

You might feel sometimes that we're far apart, but I want you to know you're always in my heart.

We've had good times and bad; our love for each other we always had.

You helped a lot in ways you don't know, and I just wanted to tell you so.

Remember the time I cried over John and me? You cried, too, and sat with me 'til I was through.

When I was in the hospital and I had to have that test that hurt me, I looked in your eye and you comforted me.

This person I cherish, I want you to know, is my sister Mary Jo.

Always remember that I love you and will always be there for you, too.

Love from your Sister Dar

Darlene S. Watson

Aunt Jack

This letter is from your niece Dar, just to tell you how nice you are.

Every time you came to visit, you'd bring me something I didn't expect. Your generosity I never forget.

The times we laughed so hard we cried, it made us feel so good inside.

The time I did your eyes because you couldn't see; it made me feel so good because you asked me.

The times we'd go out and eat, you wouldn't let me pay because you'd say, "This is my treat!"

I enjoyed the times we'd sit and talk, and had a good time when we took our walks.

The times you shared a lot with me, when we're sitting there - taking time with me shows me you care.

You talk about subjects that I didn't always know, and you'd explain them to help me grow.

You and Uncle Pat prayed for me, too; your love for me brought me through.

When you called me in the hospital and I was short with you, you understood I was sick, too.

You sent me cards to give me hope; they helped me through the times I couldn't cope.

I respect you a lot because you speak your mind; people like you are hard to find.

You stand your ground when you know you're right, and don't back down like some people might.

I admire you for what you stand for, and these are the qualities I adore.

A Story of Hate, Love, and Faith

This person I love happens to be my Aunt Jackie - who I know cares a lot about me.
Aunt Jack, I want you to know that you're in my heart wherever I go.

Love always from your Niece Dar

Dazed

I took painkillers for my back and got hooked on them. How about that?

I started taking two a day, then increased it right away.

I was taking 10 a day - two at a time - and needed to have them to feel fine.

At first, it was for pain. Then I got high each day - then the thought wouldn't go away.

I would tell the doctor I was in pain, then I'd start over again.

I was in over my head; with what I took, I could be dead.

No one knew…just me. I didn't know how to get free.

For six years, I got high - not caring about the reasons why.

I would take my mom's pills, too. She didn't know what I would do.

Then one day, I said, "NO MORE!" I felt free! What do you know?

God took the urge and pain right away. I am happy today.

I learned from this: Never say never. I didn't think I would - EVER!

I thank God for what He's done, and with Him, I have won.

I was driving on them, too. What could have happened, I didn't have a clue.

I was tempted (in my state of mind) to take things that were not mine.

If God wouldn't have watched out for me, I would have been worse off - I believe.

I can relate to those who are not set free; if God hadn't delivered me, I would have gone on to something stronger.

A Story of Hate, Love, and Faith

Have a Good Day

Pray before you start; never lose heart.

Count your blessings one by one, then you'll have so much fun!

Think of one person you can bless just to relieve their unhappiness.

Say a kind word to yourself because we, too, need help.

Smile wherever you go, so people can see your glow.

When you do all of these, you'll have a good day - wait and see!

Darlene S. Watson

Set Free

In 1996, while watching TV, the Lord used the 51st Psalm to convict me of my sins; and after He convicted me, into my heart I wanted Him to be.

In the background of this Psalm was a waterfall; that's what I remember most of all.

I don't know what was happening to me. I do know it was overwhelming.

The words I heard affected me deeply. All I could do was cry repeatedly.

I kept crying over and over again and couldn't wait for it to end.

Some time after that, I started reading the Bible regularly; that's when the Lord revealed Himself to me.

When I found out that this was real, I cried for days and fear was all I could feel.

Then days afterwards, I said, "I've got to spread the word!"

I know that I was a sinner and Jesus died on the cross in place of me to forgive me and set me free - and this is what cost Him His life on Calvary.

A Story of Hate, Love, and Faith

Jesus

Jesus is gentle and kind. He loved to heal the deaf and blind.

People don't think He's alive today to heal us, too; He likes to make us brand new.

Jesus is the Word made flesh; He came so we wouldn't be depressed.

He doesn't like it when we're down. He cheers us up 'til we come around

I wait on Him because I know I'll get His best; sometimes it's for a test.

I rest in His goodness and don't fuss, relying on Him is a must.

He heals our broken hearts; going to Him is where it starts.

He is the Way, the Truth, and Life; without Him, we wouldn't survive.

He knows what we do; He just wants us to know it, too.

I care what He thinks as I ask for advice. I do what He says - I don't think twice!

All He wants is our love and to believe. All we have to do is receive.

I'm a witness on what He's done for me. I'm out of bondage because He set me free.

When we follow Him and not man, we're built on the Rock - not sand.

I read His Word day by day. It keeps all doubts far away.

Nothing you can do can change His love for you.

He wants the best for you and me. Just believe! You'll see!

Darlene S. Watson

The Cross

The cross is where it all began - to live for God and not man.

He took our debts that we couldn't pay. When He died, our sins were washed away.

He takes away our guilt and shame; that's why we're never the same.

He was put on the cross because people hated Him so; His death was painful and slow.

He shed His blood for you and me, just so we could be set free.

He came to find people who were lost. He didn't count the cost.

He laid down His life for us; in Him we put our trust.

Jesus wants to make us feel safe and sound. We feel calm when He's around.

He has risen from the grave all because He came to save.

We read His Word and believe what it says; when we do what it says, we are blessed!

He sent the Holy Spirit to be with us so we wouldn't be alone; He is with us 'til Jesus calls us home.

We tell Him how we feel inside; He is here to be our guide.

He's our stand-by, too, when we don't know what to do.

He is also with us when the storms of life come against us.

He's lowly and gentle, too; people think the opposite is true.

He takes our burdens of today. The go away…when we pray.

Jesus is love divine. He is with us all the time.

Jesus is full of grace and truth. He will always see us through.

A Story of Hate, Love, and Faith

Faith

Faith is what's in our hearts, to be with God - not to depart.

Believing gives us joy and peace. What a feeling of release!

It's His grace that saved my soul, just so I could be made whole.

He saves us for our sakes; surrender is what it takes.

I don't have to impress God with my ways. He loves me unconditionally - always.

He helped me clean my slate of all the things inside me I hate.

God forgave me of all my sins, just so I could begin again.

He wants to be our guide and friend; He promised to be with us 'til the end.

I couldn't live on my own without Him. When He knocked on my heart, I let Him in.

It's your choice if you follow Him; without Him, chances are slim.

Jesus is God's Dear Son: He died on the cross for everyone.

We stand up for what is right. We are called to be salt and light.

We put our faith and trust in Thee; what He's done for me make me believe!

He takes our pain and our sorrow - and gives us hope for tomorrow.

He knows what's best for me. He created me, don't you see?

When we come to Jesus, we're never the same. He removes all our guilt and shame.

We make it through with love and faith. He helps in all His ways.

I know what He's done for me, and this makes me believe.

Darlene S. Watson

Hope

Hope is the anchor of our souls when the storm of life blows.
Hope is what makes us strong when everything goes wrong.
When we're depressed because we're down, hope makes us come around.
Hope is what carries us through when the storms of life come against me and you.
We believe things will get better; once we know that without God, there's nowhere to go.
If we have hope for today, then all our fears would go away.
God says to hope in Him. He will help us when things are grim.
When things are bad, I am sad. I look to God to make me glad.
Without hope, we can't cope; then we're at the end of our rope.
Hope in God to get you through. You will see He's true blue.
When we have hope, our minds are at rest; then we can do our very best.
Hope helps us with new sights. It brings us to new heights.
Hope helps us to forget the past, and God gives us peace that will last.
I have hope in God's Word; it works out the way it should.
When we have hope in God's Word, it will come to pass. It will turn our problems around - at last!
Hope helps me to not think of my mess. I look to God to be blessed.
Hope sees today with the eyes of faith. Things will get better - as we forget our mistakes.

A Story of Hate, Love, and Faith

Bless

We bless each other with our words and things; happy hearts are what they bring.

We bless so we can relieve their unhappiness.

To help someone in need, we spread kindness like seeds.

When we help the young and the old, we have hearts of gold.

When we take time to serve others we see, that's all we need when they're weak.

Helping others is what we were meant to do; sometimes it can help people be brand new.

An encouraging word we like to share because some days are hard to bear.

Look around and you'll find people need help all the time.

Take time out of your day to be kind; when we help others, we have peace of mind.

A lot of people are down on their luck; what gives them hope is a few bucks.

When people cross our paths, we find that we helped in the nick of time.

We don't know what others are going through; that's why we listen, too.

We need to help people find their way; most of the time, it's important on what we say.

It is better to give than to receive, I believe.

We help out and do our best; sometimes I think it's a test.

We need help, too, and when someone helped me, it got me through.

Darlene S. Watson

Forgiveness

Forgiveness is a choice we make - not for the person, but for our own sake.

Anger built up tears us down; it only keeps us bound.

After a while, it takes its toll. We forgive others to make us whole.

We hurt inside, and there are feelings we want to hide.

Say you're sorry right away so you don't carry it the next day.

When we forgive and do our best, then our minds are at rest.

Forgiveness is hard at first to do; with God's help, we can see it through.

We can extend our hearts to understand, to freely forgive our fellow man.

There are so many things that hurt us in the past; when we forgive, we're free at last!

We show love for each other when we forgive our sisters and brothers.

We think we are hurting them; all it does is hurt us in the end.

When we hurt others, we want to be forgiven, too; that's why we forgive what others do.

We need to bring Salvation back so we can see that no one is better than you and me.

We need to forgive ourselves, too, from all the things we used to do.

We know what we have done, and it's not the same for everyone.

So be good to yourself because we, too, need help.

A Story of Hate, Love, and Faith

Begin Again

Salvation is free to us; all we have to do it trust.

Jesus died to set us free; all He wants is for us to believe.

He has always loved us from the start - always with us, never to depart.

Our sins are gone when He forgives. He really cares how we live.

He came to Earth to show us how to live - not to be selfish, but to give.

Love is what He's about; when we love each other, we have no doubt.

He is good to you and me. Everything we have is from Thee.

We pray to Him when things are bad; when He answers our prayers, we are glad.

Grace is a gift to us; all we have to do is accept and trust.

He heals our hearts and our minds; we become new over time.

There is power in His name; when we give Him our lives, we're never the same.

We know God is real by what we see. This is what makes us believe.

He came to set things right: He takes us to new heights.

God created Heaven and Earth; when we are saved, we have a new birth.

We need to be forgive for our sins; that's why we need to open our hearts and let Him in.

God loves us with an everlasting love; that's why He came from above.

He came so we would know how much He loves us so.

What we deserved, He took on Himself - just so we wouldn't go to Hell.

Darlene S. Watson

Grace

Grace is a free gift to us. All we have to do is believe and trust.
He died to set us free from our sins; we just need to let Him in.
When He forgives us of our sins, a new life in Him begins.
Being led by God's grace sets us free to love each other the way He loves you and me.
Grow in grace and the knowledge of the Lord; He is the only one we adore.
Grace is power from on high so we can live right in God's eyes.
So we could have eternal life, He made the ultimate sacrifice.
We were dead in trespasses and sin; by His Spirit we're made to live again.
I pray for grace to get me through each day, and He strengthens me to go His way.
He guides me in what I should do. I find He is true blue.
I can trust Him to show me the way. I call on Him always.
We can't do anything without His grace; He sends His Holy Spirit in His place.
He gives us peace inside. His Spirit is our guide.
He works in quietness - without strife. We need Him in our life.

A Story of Hate, Love, and Faith

Mercy

Mercy is what we don't deserve. Without it, it would be hard to endure.

When we do wrong, mercy we plead. It's new every morning for you and me.

God shows us mercy when we confess; when we do, our minds are at rest.

We can tell when He shows us mercy: the guilt of our sins leaves us.

We need to show mercy that we received so that we can be relieved.

It's right to do, and it is good in God's sight, too.

Mercy is what we need each day so all our sins are washed away.

When God corrects us, we don't feel condemned. We can always begin again.

When we do wrong, we need mercy to clean our slates to get back on track and to go forward - not look back.

We have a fresh start each day when we go to God always.

God freely gives us mercy when we need it. We need to receive it - and believe it!

Extend your heart and hand; most of all, understand.

Mercy is God's compassionate side. We know we can come to Him and not hide.

Mercy helps us do our best - not to make us feel less and less.

We all make mistakes in our lives; without God's mercy, we wouldn't survive.

Mercy is one thing we can't do without. We all make mistakes - without a doubt.

Darlene S. Watson

Joy

Joy is a calm delight to make us happy and not uptight.
In God's presence is fullness of joy.
Joy is what we receive when we believe.
Peace and joy are in our hearts; this is where it all starts.
It is the Fruit of the Spirit that grows slow, but when it is developed, you will know.
When we choose to be happy, joy begins; it's not on the outside, but within.
We need to be positive and think the best; when we do, we are blessed.
We need to renew our minds with God's thoughts; it takes away all our doubts.
Joy is one thing I don't want to lose because then I think, "What's the use?"
Joy gets us through so we can feel happy and not blue.
Joy is what makes us laugh; we feel better to finish our tasks.
Enjoying life every day keeps the gloom away.
We all have burdens to bear. We feel much better when someone is there.
Bad thoughts make us feel crappy; when we share, we are happy!
Lift up your head when it hands down. Laughing a lot brings us around.
We need to laugh at ourselves, too; it always feels good to do.

A Story of Hate, Love, and Faith

Peace

Peace is God's power; we need it every hour.

When storms blow and we're upset, we try to stay peaceful instead.

Peace is the power to keep us still when we do God's will.

Peace is beyond our understanding to us. What gives us peace is our trust.

Peace is what we need in our minds. When it's God's peace, that's a sure sign.

Peace comes when we do our best to believe our minds are at rest.

Peace is like a river stream that is quiet and serene.

I had to stay calm over and over again to let it grow. Now I have it, I won't let it go!

We walk in peace, not strife. We must have it in our lives.

First, we make peace with God and agree with Him; then our peace begins.

Peace is like a river that flows. How we have it, no one knows.

Jesus said His peace He leaves with us so we would know that He's with us wherever we go.

You can't find it any other way. We need to call on Jesus right away.

He comes to reside in our hearts - never to depart.

Only He is our peace; when we give Him our lives, what a release!

Darlene S. Watson

Jesus Christ

Jesus is the One; He is God's Dear Son.

Jesus died to set us free; that was why He was nailed to a tree.

He is humble, meek, and mild. We come to Him like a child.

He rose on the third day and went back to Heaven - far away.

He's alive and real, too; He's coming back very soon.

Jesus says, "I'm the Way, the Truth, and the Life." We come to Him get a new life.

Jesus said, "The truth will set you free. To live a good life, you have to follow Me."

Jesus is divine and man, too; He came in the flesh to feel the way we do.

Jesus is the same yesterday, today, and tomorrow; He's the one I want to follow.

He has our best interests at heart; He loved us from the start.

In Him, I have eternal life. Because I put my trust in Him, I will never die.

His mercy is new every morning for us to receive. I need it a lot - believe me!

Jesus shed His blood on a cross to set us free; it cost Him dearly.

People hated Him in His days; they didn't accept Him like they should.

He came to save and not condemn; we need to open our hearts and let Him in.

His Word is who He is. Believe it so you can live.

They are spirit and life - and true, too. When we trust in His Word, He will see us through.

He died on the cross just so he could save all of us.

He laid His life down so we could live again and to forgive us of our sins.

A Story of Hate, Love, and Faith

Holy Spirit

The Spirit of the Lord is a gentleman. He's the one God has sent.
He's our teacher and our guide; He helps us in our lives.
He's our stand-by; He helps us when we try.
He gives us power to do with ease. What a release!
He helps us do God's will. We need to be Spirit-filled.
He's my friend, too; He helps me think things through.
With His grace, He makes me strong - not to do things wrong.
He comforts me when I'm down and cheers me up 'til I come around.
He encourages me to keep going; He helps me to keep growing.
When I ask for wisdom on what to do, He always tells, too!
I walk in the Spirit and not the flesh; when I do, my mind's at rest.
I pray throughout my day, and this keeps the devil away.
He gives me grace to meet each need and gives me the faith to believe.
When I do wrong, I come to Him; He forgives time and time again.
Jesus gave Him to us in His place; He gives us strength for the things we face.
He doesn't force us to go His way. He gives us a choice always.
He gives us a choice to listen to His voice.
I walk with Him to keep me on track. He helps me see what I lack.
He's as gentle as a dove and always helps us out of love.

Darlene S. Watson

My Way

No more will I live a lie. If no one can accept that, BYE-BYE!

I'll see people for who they are; the most important is me - Dar.

There are things I will say; if you don't like the truth, get out the way!

I am who I am and can't change that. I don't want to - and that's a fact!

No more will I play the part just because you don't want to make a clean start.

I will think before I speak and choose my words well. When I'm asked, I will tell.

I will not judge because who am I to say? I expect you to treat me the same way.

It's my God-given right to be happy; I won't be around people who make me feel unhappy.

I will be around people who care about me - and if they don't, I'll let them free.

I have my limits and won't go too far; for once in my life, I'm thinking of Dar.

I'm the only one I got, so I have to think of me and not let people do what they please with my feelings.

I will help people whenever I can; if it's for the wrong reason, I'll make a stand.

I feel good and I want to stay that way, and for me, the only way is to pray.

When people can't move because they won't let go of the past, don't take it out on me when you want to blast.

Don't take it out on me because you're not happy. It's up to you to change you - not me.

If something isn't right, I'll intervene - and if it's too heavy, I'm out of that scene.

I can only fix myself - not you; so don't expect me to.

When I accept the things I can't change or undo, then I move on to something new.

A Story of Hate, Love, and Faith

I will do my best to live right and always with God in sight.

I will love myself as God loves me and will believe in me.

I will let God guide me in all ways and set an example through all my days.

Accept the things you can't change, but always try to do your best while you're still alive...

Darlene S. Watson

Hidden

We are all looking for things to make us feel good. We need to know where to look. God is the one who knows what's true.

Most of the time, I feel fine. Then there are days that aren't that good. I sit still and listen to my heart so I can hear what myself thinks. After a while, words start to come; then I know what has made me feel down. As soon as I can identify what's wrong with me, then I feel free. Sometimes it takes days to know what the problem is, but I keep at it until I am better. It's part of me that is hidden and when I search for the answer, it is given. Not every day is alike, but every day I have peace and joy. I keep my mind focused on God and by doing this, my mind is at rest. A relationship with God grows each day. The more you know Him, the more you trust. You have to read His Word each day so that you can keep the darkness away. It builds our faith up, too, and makes us strong. We know how to live in God's sight because His Word is our light. God's Word is true and it really works. It heals our souls. When we spend time with God, we start to think like He does. He forms us into His Dear Son, and that's so Jesus can live His life through us. When you surrender all that you are, then you get His life living in you. I feel more like living than I ever did before - that's because I'm born again! I will go to Heaven when I die and will live forever with God. This can also be for you if you make the choice to listen to God instead of the world.

A Story of Hate, Love, and Faith

As you walk each day with God, you become closer to Him and notice He's around - a lot. The devil blinds our minds to the truth and only God can make us understand. All the 'Ds' are from Satan. Just think of these: Depression. Despair. Death. Danger. Darkness. Discouragement. Disappointment. Disturbed…and I could go on and on. They all start with the letter 'D': 'D' for devil. I had headaches most of the time because I was so angry. I stuffed that away, too, so no one knew. I accept who God created me to be and that has set me free to be all that I can be!

Darlene S. Watson

Set Free

I was so messed up in my life. Through faith and trust in the Lord, I've made it through. It all starts there, and then He begins to show me what is keeping me stuck or sick. I was scared to know what was there. These are things I never shared. It was too painful to go through, but over time, I felt brand new. I convinced myself by my thoughts that I would always be this way. Jesus came to set me free. All I had to do was surrender me! God has always kept me going, even when I didn't think I'd make it. He never gave up on me. He stayed with me 'til I was free. I had to face all the junk that was inside of me. God told me that I had to go through it to get through it. The devil wants us to hide what's there so we can stay in bondage. Jesus is the light that says the truth will set you free. When God exposed all my sins, it was hard to take. He kept it up for my sake. He wanted me to break free and live a life of victory. I am glad I know what truth is and to expose what held me in pain.

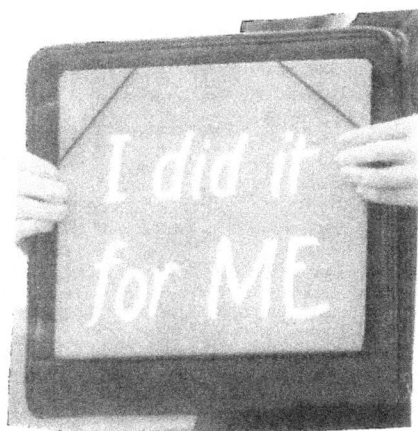

I did it for ME

To get WELL GooD Life!

Darlene S. Watson

Reflecting

It's been six years since this horror began. Once the memories started, I couldn't make them stop.

I relived most of that abuse all over again during these years. I shed an awful number of tears.

What really broke my heart was to face the fact that my whole life was a farce - and the people I loved didn't love me.

These poems saved my life because after each one, I went through. God gave me the gift to write it through.

That's what saved my sanity: writing out what was inside of me.

These stories are my healing because when they came out, I got stronger and better over time - and today, I am doing fine.

I really thought my family was average. Never in my wildest dreams did I know any of this. Now I know why I've been sick all my life…it all fits.

I've come to know God even more and have finally found peace in my soul. God has made me whole.

When I forgave the people who did these things to me, I felt healing inside of me.

It wasn't so important to me who they were; all I cared about was getting cured.

I was crippled in a lot of areas in my life and I wanted to find out why.

I searched all my life for answers, but it wasn't until God came into my life did these things come out.

God says, "If you seek, you will find". He will give us answers in time.

That's what He did for me…I believe.

One thing they didn't accomplish was to drive me insane; they are to blame all the same.

They messed with my mind a lot; pain and suffering is what I got.

A Story of Hate, Love, and Faith

God says the heart of a man is what counts; they tried to take God out of my heart from the start.

I look to God to help me stay strong, and not to focus on what went wrong.

MY. liFe NOW

I am stronger

CALM IN the

SPIRIT

A Story of Hate, Love, and Faith

QUICK ORDER FORM

Satisfaction guaranteed

Email orders: BestSeller@PearlyGatesPublishing.com

Telephone orders: Call 1-832-319-3970. Have credit card ready.

Postal orders: Mail payment in full to Pearly Gates Publishing LLC, P.O. Box 62287, Houston, TX 77205

Please send _____ copy(ies) of "*A Story of Hate, Love, and Faith*" for $12.99 each (plus tax and S/H) to the address listed below.
Tax: 8% of subtotal / book(s)
S/H: U.S. Priority Mail with Tracking - $9.00 up to two copies; $18.00 for three to eight copies; $23.00 for nine to 15 copies. *For bulk orders above 15, please call the number listed for telephone orders to inquire about the discount.*

Name:
Address:
City, State, Zip Code:
Telephone:
Email:

Payment Amount Enclosed (USD only): $ _____
Check # (Payable to Angela R. Edwards, CEO):

Money Order #:

Credit Card *(Visa, MasterCard, AMEX, Discover)*
Name on card:
Card Number:
Exp. Date:
Security Code (located on rear of card in signature area):

Pearly Gates Publishing LLC

"Inspiring Christian Authors to BE Authors"

QUICK ORDER FORM

Satisfaction guaranteed

Email orders: BestSeller@PearlyGatesPublishing.com

Telephone orders: Call 1-832-319-3970. Have credit card ready.

Postal orders: Mail payment in full to Pearly Gates Publishing LLC, P.O. Box 62287, Houston, TX 77205

Please send _____ copy(ies) of "*A Story of Hate, Love, and Faith*" for $12.99 each (plus tax and S/H) to the address listed below.
Tax: 8% of subtotal / book(s)
S/H: U.S. Priority Mail with Tracking - $9.00 up to two copies; $18.00 for three to eight copies; $23.00 for nine to 15 copies. *For bulk orders above 15, please call the number listed for telephone orders to inquire about the discount.*

Name:
Address:
City, State, Zip Code:
Telephone:
Email:

Payment Amount Enclosed (USD only): $ _____
Check # (Payable to Angela R. Edwards, CEO):

Money Order #:

Credit Card *(Visa, MasterCard, AMEX, Discover)*
Name on card:
Card Number:
Exp. Date:
Security Code (located on rear of card in signature area):

Pearly Gates Publishing LLC

"Inspiring Christian Authors to BE Authors"

www.ingramcontent.com/pod-product-compliance
Lightning Source LLC
Chambersburg PA
CBHW081148090426
42736CB00017B/3236